"If you live with depression or anxiety and are looking for an alternative or additional support to medication intervention, this book is a bedside read; inspirational, directional, empowering, and a spiritual guide to finding strength within oneself and applying that strength to everyday functions in life. Cognitive changes and positive thinking are the keys to making the change you seek. You can make the difference within yourself with simple life-changing methods provided by the experience and guidance of an author who knows. She searched within herself and her Savior and found the light, and now she is sharing it with you. You make the choice to stay in the dark or live in the light."

—**Kristy Lee Cropper**, LPC

"Living in the Light provides an engaging mix of contemporary wisdom, personal experience, professional perspective, and scriptural insight into the challenges of dealing with depression. The premise of changing lives by changing thoughts and taking action to improve in very specific ways, if applied, will undoubtedly have a positive impact in the lives of readers."

—**Donna Lister**, PhD (c), MSN, APRN, FNP-BC, associate professor, Nursing Department Chair, SUU

"As a physician, bishop, and father, I have frequently encountered individuals who struggle with depression and anxiety. *Living in the Light* is the only practical guide I have seen for overcoming these challenging conditions. This is a powerful resource for those searching for a way out from under these burdens as well as for those dealing with the normal stressors in life. I am convinced a happier, more peaceful life awaits those who will faithfully follow the steps presented in *Living in the Light."*

—**David C. Smith**, DO, LDS bishop, father of eight, emergency medicine physician

"Mrs. West invites us to follow her personal journey into understanding the individual, clinical, and deeply spiritual aspects of rising above depression. Though each person's challenges are unique, each reader will greatly benefit from her study. Her invitation to "walk in the Light" is well grounded in scriptures and clinical recommendations. Above all, she provides actionable exercises helping empower readers to regain control of their symptoms. A great resource for patients, counselors, clergies, and loved ones."

—**Jon Vashaw**, MPAS, PA-C

"Living in the Light gives a glimpse into the darkness of suffering from depression and, more important, it provides practical ways to overcome the darkness and return to living in the light. The author's personal story of strength provides inspiration to each reader. This book uses accepted medical knowledge,

scriptural insight, and common sense to guide the reader to a better place. I have read many books over the years on this subject and I greatly appreciate Lacey West's emphasis on the Atonement in overcoming depression and anxiety. I look forward to recommending this book to my friends, colleagues, and patients."

—**Matthew West**, BCHS, PA-C, NREMT-P

"This book is an excellent resource, workbook, and guide for anyone suffering from depression. All of the major symptoms of depression are covered, and ways to deal with them are explored."

—**Amber Lingard**, CSW

"Living in the Light is not only a great resource for battling depression but also a source of better understanding for anyone who might have a loved one battling these demons. It takes a spiritual as well as a physiological approach to the treatment of depression, encompassing the person as whole, which in my experience always achieves better results."

—**Cody Nielson**, MS, PA-C

"The strength of West's book *Living in the Light*, is the straightforward application to deal with negative thoughts and depression. She presents some great insights and tools to help guide people to be happier and healthy."

—**Chaplain (Major) Gaylan R. Springer**, Headquarters Battery, 2nd Battalion, 222nd Field Artillery

"A must-read for individuals struggling with depression and or anxiety! As a therapist, I have found this book to be a wonderful addition to the therapy clients receive from my practice. It is written with an interesting mix of research and evidenced-based treatments as well as first hand personal experience that gives the reader actual tools and hope that recovery is possible. The author has done an expert job of weaving emotional, cognitive, behavioral, and spiritual approaches to working with the challenges that come as a result of depression and anxiety. It is now on my recommended reading list for patients in my practice."

—**Dean F. Anderson**, LCSW, private practitioner and director, Adult Outpatient Services Wasatch Mental Health, Provo, Utah

"Living in the Light is a uniquely candid book depicting reality for many silent sufferers of depression. Lacey West offers simple and practical insights to assist individuals overcoming the debilitating effects of depression and supports them with a gentle blend of common sense and scientific research. A meaningful true story offering sensible advice and expertise for anyone willing to obtain help with their struggles from depression."

—**Thane R. Goodrich**, PhD

Living

IN THE

Light

LACEY A. WEST, RN, BSN
GARY L ANDERSON, MS, CMHC

CFI

An Imprint of Cedar Fort, Inc.
Springville, Utah

DISCLAIMER

This book is designed to provide general information only and is not intended to assist individuals with serious mental health concerns or illnesses such as bipolar disorder or schizophrenia, or to replace the advice of a doctor or mental health professional. Therefore, neither the author nor the publisher accepts liability, express or implied, for damages of any kind not limited to, consequential damages. This book should only be used as a guide and for informational purposes and not as legal or other professional advice. The author and publisher encourage the reader to consult with a doctor or an appropriate professional. This book does not contain all information available on depression and anxiety. The material presented cannot be individualized; therefore, it may not be applicable in every way or to every person. This book should serve only as a guide to assist you in overcoming discouragement, not as a substitute for professional assistance. All examples depicted in the text are experiences from real people. Names have been changed to protect the identity of those represented. If at any time you have thoughts of self-harm, consult a healthcare professional immediately.

This is not an official publication of The Church of Jesus Christ of Latter-day Saints. The opinions and views expressed herein belong solely to the author and do not necessarily represent the opinions or views of Cedar Fort, Inc. Permission for the use of sources, graphics, and photos is also solely the responsibility of the author.

ISBN 13: 978-1-4621-1148-0

Published by CFI, an imprint of Cedar Fort, Inc.
2373 W. 700 S., Springville, UT 84663
Distributed by Cedar Fort, Inc., www.cedarfort.com

LIBRARY OF CONGRESS CATALOGING-IN-PUBLICATION DATA

West, Lacey A., 1986- author.
  Living in the light : how to fight the darkness of depression and anxiety / Lacey A. West and Gary L Anderson.
      pages cm
  Includes bibliographical references and index.
  ISBN 978-1-4621-1148-0 (alk. paper)
  1. Depression, Mental--Religious aspects--Church of Jesus Christ of Latter-day Saints. 2. Depression, Mental--Treatment. 3. Depressed persons--Religious life. I. Anderson, Gary L, 1969- author. II. Title.

  BX8643.D44W47 2013
  248.8'625--dc23

                    2012041845

Cover design by Erica Dixon
Cover design © 2012 Lyle Mortimer
Edited and typeset by Emily S. Chambers

Printed in the United States of America

10 9 8 7 6 5 4 3 2 1

Printed on acid-free paper

For my mother—who gave me hope when I had none. And for my husband—who loves me unconditionally in spite of my weaknesses.

Contents

The first words of the Bible are: "In the beginning God created the heaven and the earth. And the earth was without form, and void; and darkness was upon the face of the deep. And the Spirit of God moved upon the face of the waters. And God said, Let there be light: and there was light. And God saw the light, that it was good: and God divided the light from the darkness" (Gen. 1:1–4). We note from this scripture that God knew there must be light, for light was good, and he divided the light from the darkness.[1]

—N. Eldon Tanner

Authors' Note

I would like to clearly state my position as author of these words. I am by no means a psychologist, therapist, or religious expert. I am merely a wife, mother, and nurse—as average as they come—who suffered from an illness or problem known as depression. I do not claim to understand completely the physical, mental, or religious aspects of this disease, nor do I profess to acknowledge this text as doctrine. As a member of the LDS faith, I must exclaim that the following words are my own and are not necessarily the teachings of The Church of Jesus Christ of Latter-day Saints; however, I pray that my words are in harmony with its teachings.

A majority of the ideas expressed in this book are thoughts from my family, teachings from the scriptures, cognitive therapies, and my own life experiences. I wish to express gratitude to my friends Danielle and Christian; my mother, Terilyn; my sister, Nicole; my uncle, Thane; and my husband, Jared. I appreciate all your advice, editing, love, and support. A special thank you to my uncle Gary, for sharing his expertise to make this book a reality.

In my own quest for happiness and freedom from depression along with my experience as a registered nurse, I have come across insightful information that has enriched my life and enabled me with the skills to rise above discouragement. My only intent in writing this book is to give to others what I have been so richly blessed to discover.

—**Lacey A. West**, BSN, RN

Whehen I was first approached to support Lacey in coauthoring a book, I was unaware of her history and struggle with depression. As I read through her text, I was keenly impressed with how she has summarized and presented key ideas in understanding and overcoming depression. I found that her stories and examples were surprisingly similar to the ones I have experienced with my own clients. As I would read her counsel to take action in one way or another, I found myself saying, "Hey, that is just what I recommend to my clients as well."

I have worked in the mental health field for over fifteen years. My experience includes work in schools, in public and private agencies, and with individuals and families. Much of my work has been with teens through residential behavioral treatment settings. My clients range from ages six to over seventy. I currently own and operate my own practice, providing mental health services in a rural community. It is my hope that I can support Lacey's work from the perspective of a mental health professional. I have contributed all of the "Professional Insights" sections within the following text.

One of the challenges of counseling others is guiding them to a true understanding of the problem, helping them recognize their own contributions to the problem, and then having them acknowledge their part in the solution. *Living in the Light* will guide you through these essential steps to recovery. There are examples throughout the book of experiences from real clients I have counseled who have gone through this process. Their names have been changed for confidentiality purposes. Throughout the book are a number of "Take Action" sections. I would encourage you to be active. Reading about an illness will not help you overcome the illness any more than watching an exercise video will help you become more physically fit. You have to do something. The smallest steps, no matter how small, are far more powerful than the grandest good intentions.

There is nothing more rewarding than assisting someone in the process of overcoming discouragement. God bless you in your journey to happiness.

—**Gary L Anderson**, MS, CMHC

Part One

ILLUMINATE THE MIND

Chapter One

DEPRESSION—IS IT REAL?

"In the quiet heart is hidden sorrow that the eye can't see."[2]
—Hymn no. 220

For all human beings there has been and will always be an ongoing pursuit of happiness. It's as if our very DNA yearns for it. A young child seeks after things that bring him pleasure, like candy, toys, and praise. If you ask any adult what they want most, you usually find they just want to be happy. Their answer might come in the form of a worldly treasure such as a new car or a bigger paycheck. But the underlying desire behind the object is the thought, *This new car will make me happy.* Why do some people find it so difficult to obtain the happiness they want most?

The gospel of Jesus Christ teaches us that "men are that they might have joy" (2 Nephi 2:25). We can assume that women are included in this statement as well. Yet this life, although wonderful, is far from absolute bliss. We knew this from our life before earth. As we dwelled in the premortal existence, the challenges that we would face in mortality were explained to us. We knew, at least to some extent, what we were getting into. (In medicine we call this *informed consent.*) We used our precious agency when we chose to come to earth. Birth meant entering into a battlefield of sin, death, natural disasters, heartache, and pain. Can joy be experienced by someone living in such a world? What does the scripture in 2 Nephi imply? Does it mean that men are that they *might* have joy every once in a while? Or does it entail that we *might* experience joy but we *might* not? These are questions I have asked

3

myself in my own struggle for happiness—a fight through a dark battle of depression.

You may have decided to read this book because you also suffer from these dark feelings, you may be a loved one of someone who suffers, or you may just be interested in what *Living in the Light* is all about. Whatever the case may be, I ask that you have an open mind as I relate to you my personal acquaintance with the monster of depression. Following, we can discuss the illness and then the underlying question, "Is it possible for all men (and women) to have joy?" Not just the happy, bubbly people, or the rich or skinny people, but *all* people; even people like me who are prone to negative thoughts? I am here to tell you that it *is* possible, and I'll share what I've learned to make it so. But first, it's story time.

Once upon a time, there was a young girl from a small town in Utah. She was plain, a little tall for her age, and raised in a good LDS home. She had a love for horses, country life, and her family. She had always been good-natured and slightly shy, and she had an easily offended spirit. All she wanted to do was make her parents proud. This young girl had a wonderful childhood, full of loving memories with family and friends.

One day her father brought home an old pony he had purchased at an auction for an extremely low price. The pony was so small and old that no one else was willing to purchase him; but to this little girl, the pony became the love of her life. She would ride him all by herself through the rich alfalfa fields, her blonde pigtails bouncing with each step. For several years, this special bond between girl and horse existed perfectly; he was her truest friend.

One winter was especially cold and stormy. Her mother and father noticed the old pony wearing down and were discussing the matter in the kitchen one night when the little girl overheard them. A knot began to develop in her stomach, and each night before she went to bed she would toss and turn with frightening dreams. First thing in the morning, she would run out into the yard and check on the pony. She was afraid that one morning she would awake to find him dead.

Sometimes the little girl would stare out her bedroom window toward the horse corral and try not to cry. The gray winter sky was so cold, and her pony looked so old and frail standing in the deep snow. She tried to explain to her mother how she felt, but the only explanation she could muster was that she felt as if something horrible was about to happen though she didn't know why (she later discovered this was a symptom known as *impending doom*). The winter went on in this same fashion, and each night, the knot in her stomach grew worse.

One cold gray morning, to her horror, she discovered her little old pony lying on his side. Her mom said that he was an old horse and probably had pneumonia, but the little girl didn't know what that meant. She only knew that her best friend was sick and drifting from her. Her mother sent her to school, telling the girl that she would care for the pony and let her know if anything happened. Throughout the day, the knot in her stomach intensified. After lunch, her mother came and pulled her out of her little third-grade classroom into the empty hallway. Without being told, the girl knew what had happened. Her mom didn't say anything; she just held her close, and together they cried.

If it wasn't obvious, this little girl was me, and this was the first episode of depression that I can remember. It was preceded by months of anxiety. You were probably expecting something quite different. Perhaps you expected me to relate some traumatic death of a relative, a natural disaster, or even a horrible family relationship that made me that way. But the irony of depression is that it comes to average people with seemingly happy lives as well as to people that you might expect to be depressed. It is real. Each person may classify it differently, but it is as real as the sky is blue, and it affects thousands of lives throughout the world.

Jack Challem, author of *The Food-Mood Solution*, gives the following statistics on the occurrence of depression. "Recent articles in the *Archives of General Psychiatry*, published by the American Medical Association, have pointed out that at least *one of every two people* will experience a serious mood or mental health problem at some time in his or her life . . . *One in five people* will suffer from serious depression or bipolar (manic-depressive) disorder."[3]

Although depression is extremely common, at this early point in my life, I didn't recognize what I was feeling. During the few months that surrounded my pony's death, I felt completely dark and discouraged. And would it not be unusual if I hadn't? You might be thinking to yourself that any young girl in the same situation would feel the same way; however, after the death of my pony, the pain didn't ease up, and it didn't get better with time. In fact, it got worse. From that time on, every morning I would wake up with the same dark, gut-wrenching feeling. Eventually I did recover from the loss of my pony, but the gloomy feeling never went away, and that hopeless sensation became the focus of my attention. A key note to remember about depression is that it is *prolonged* unhappiness, and it *interrupts* the flow of daily life. I knew something was different with me when the sadness never went away. It had become my shadow.

At the age of twelve, I watched as cancer slowly took my grandmother away from me. Although this was difficult at the time, the pain should have lessened after several weeks or months, but instead the dark feelings escalated. My life was not terrible; in fact, it was probably more blissful than many others', but I had a difficult time feeling it. Once my mother and I realized that this sadness wasn't going away *even after the hardships had passed,* we decided to make an appointment with our family physician. I was then diagnosed with depression. Finally there was a word to describe what I was experiencing. The doctor explained that the pain from a broken bone was visible to other people, and although depression hurt just as badly, it was hidden deep inside—invisible to people around me. That is what makes it so difficult to accept. Most diseases at least allow a person to hope, but in this instance, the disease is a hope crusher. This creates a real problem. I had it set in my mind that I was just a sad, dark, weak person who could not handle anything. My first step to recovery was finally realizing that what I was experiencing was real, and that there were other people who felt the same. After many years of medications, faith, prayers, and cognitive therapies, I'm here to tell you that it has been an extensive and difficult journey, but I have come a long way and I want to assist you in this recovery process.

One Saturday morning, after reading a chapter from the New Testament about Christ's ministry, I had a profound idea. I thought, *If the Savior can heal all these people, He can heal me. I know He can. I have faith.* With that I ran downstairs and asked my father for a priesthood blessing. With all the faith in my fourteen-year-old heart, I told him that because he would use God's priesthood power in his blessing, he could make my depression disappear forever. Looking back, I wonder what went through his mind. Of the many blessings my father gave me, this one remains everlasting in my mind. With only the small audience of my mother, he rested his large, gentle hands upon my head and blessed me with God's power. During the blessing, I distinctly remember hearing him say, " . . . and your depression will cease." My heart leapt for joy at these words. I instantly felt better and thought, *This is it, I knew he could heal me! I should have done this years ago!* It was only a few hours later that the feelings came back. I started to doubt as quickly as I had mustered up my faith. I began to think that my father only told me what I wanted to hear instead of what the Spirit told him to say. I apologize publicly now for thinking such a thing. My father is a wonderful man who did follow the Holy Ghost. I just had to learn, like many people do, that answers to prayers and blessings often come in ways we don't expect. He didn't bless me that the depression would cease immediately, but he did bless me that it would in fact cease. Once I realized that I must search, pray, and thirst for a cure, day by day, my blessing was fulfilled. I believe it was this drive inside me to find the answer of how to make the healing complete that allowed for me to keep pushing and searching until I felt I had overcome this dark monster. I didn't give up because I knew the Lord had spoken, and I knew the Lord could not lie (Enos 1:6).

According to the Mental Health Review Module by Assessment Technologies Institute, women are more likely to have depression than men.[4] While this appears to be true according to those I associate with, many men are worn down by depression as well. Because of the "tough guy" image men are often expected to have, perhaps they are more hesitant about disclosing their condition.

I believe that religious individuals may be especially prone to discouragement. With covenants to honor, commandments to obey, and lessons and talks to prepare, it is easy to get discouraged. It is easy to become overwhelmed by the guilt of wrongly assuming you are not measuring up. All of these expectations placed upon us can more easily be met with the grace of our Savior who makes up the difference of what we cannot do; however, in this busy world it is easy to forget His gift. It is easy to take the weight of the entire world upon your shoulders until you are squished like a little bug. Not only does the world place stressful burdens upon us, but a lot of the expectations that add pressure to life are unnecessarily self-imposed.

Satan also works overtime on faithful Christians. Why would he need to tempt or discourage those who are already not following the doctrine of Christ? He hurls discouragement at stalwart Saints, hoping to batter them down to the point of forgetting, or not believing, their self-worth. If one forgets he or she is a child of God, it really only goes downhill from there. Batter us he will, but he will not—he cannot—bring us down unless we let him.

Please know that you are not weak if you have depression. In fact, it means that you care. You just might care a little too much about the wrong things. You are placing burdens upon yourself that you don't need to carry; but you are a good, spiritually sensitive, kind person. And you can be all those things and happy too. It's possible.

Professional Insights

My visits with new clients usually begin with a brief discussion about confidentiality and the limits of that confidentiality regarding issues of safety. "What brings you in today?" becomes my next question if I haven't already gained that information when setting up the appointment. Common expressions include: "I am not sleeping well," "I can't seem to focus," "I am not getting along with my spouse," or "I can't shake this feeling of dread." The process of assessment is one of "question and answer" dialogue. Sometimes the client knows quite well what is wrong, but often they only feel that something is not right—but aren't quite sure what it is.

As I ask more and more questions about what they are experiencing, it becomes clear that their symptoms are consistent with depression. What continues to be a somewhat surprising experience for me is seeing how comforted they seem when I explain to them that there is a name for what they are experiencing. As I clarify that the combination of physical and emotional symptoms they have described are consistent with a diagnosis of depression, a surprising look of relief is revealed. I have come to find that when they simply realize that depression is real, and that they are not alone—that others have experienced this darkness—they are reassured. Plus they experience added comfort in understanding that it most definitely can be overcome.

NOTES

1. N. Eldon Tanner, "The Light of the Gospel," *Ensign*, Nov. 1977, 49.

2. "Lord, I Would Follow Thee," *Hymns of the Church of Jesus Christ of Latter-day Saints* (Salt Lake City, UT: The Church of Jesus Christ of Latter-day Saints, 1985), no. 220.

3. Jack Challem and Melvyn R. Werbach, MD, *The Food-Mood Solution: All-Natural Ways to Banish Anxiety, Depression, Anger, Stress, Overeating, and Alcohol and Drug Problems—and Feel Good Again* (Hoboken, NJ: John Wiley & Sons, 2007), 3; emphasis added.

4. Lucindra Campbell, APRN, PhD, BC et al., *Mental Health Nursing Care*, Review Module Edition 6.1 (Overland Park, KS: Assessment Technologies Institute, LLC, 2006), 146.

Chapter Two

WHAT IS DEPRESSION?

If you are reading this because you feel you might have depression, I want you to read through the following list and compare your symptoms to it. If you are reading this for any other reason, recognize that the symptoms below are how people who suffer from depression feel. This list is taken from the book, *Overcoming Depression*, by doctors Demitri and Janice Papolos.[1]

Signs and Symptoms of Depression

- Depressed or irritable or anxious mood
- Poor appetite and weight loss, or the opposite, increased appetite and weight gain
- Sleep disturbance: sleeping too little or sleeping too much in an irregular pattern
- Loss of energy: excessive fatigue or tiredness
- Change in activity level, either increased or decreased
- Loss of interest or pleasure in usual activities
- Decreased sexual drive
- Physical aches and pains
- Diminished ability to think or concentrate
- Feelings of worthlessness or excessive guilt that may reach grossly unreasonable or delusional proportions
- Other psychotic or delusional thinking
- Recurrent thoughts of death or self-harm; wishing to be dead or contemplating or attempting suicide

Often depression and anxiety go hand in hand. You may have felt depressed along with some of these symptoms of anxiety outlined by Dr. Edmund J. Bourne in his book, *The Anxiety and Phobia Workbook.*[2]

Signs and Symptoms of Anxiety

- Shortness of breath
- Heart palpitations (rapid or irregular heartbeat)
- Trembling or shaking
- Sweating
- Choking
- Nausea or abdominal distress
- Numbness
- Dizziness or unsteadiness
- Feeling of detachment or being out of touch with yourself
- Hot flashes or chills
- Fear of dying
- Fear of going crazy or out of control

Discouragement is a real issue attacking people across the globe. To be able to fight against it, it is beneficial to first understand what is going on inside the body that causes, or is related to, discouragement. What could cause such horrible feelings? Are some people born with a chemical imbalance, or are some people really just gloomy? Do some people make it up, or do some people just have negative personalities? In all honesty, science does not have all the exact answers to these questions. Several theories have been introduced about how and why people feel gloomy. It is understood that chemical exchanges *do* occur in the brain, but is it these chemicals alone that actually cause mood alterations? Whatever happens on a cellular level is not as important to me as the things we *have* learned that directly correlate with depression and anxiety—one of these being our thoughts. A renowned doctor of psychiatry, Dr. David Burns states, "All your moods are created by your 'cognitions,' or thoughts. A cognition refers to the way you look at things—your perceptions, mental attitudes, and beliefs."[3]

I will give an example to illustrate how our thoughts control our mood. Suppose a certain young man—let's call him Jason—is having a BBQ with his roommates. They are all enjoying the beginning of summer break following their first year of college. They are having fun, laughing and throwing a football around. Someone yells over to the other guys and says, "Hey our grades are posted!"

Jason makes his way over to his friend's laptop and pulls up his grades. He is horrified at seeing a few Bs and one C. The grades were much lower than he anticipated. Immediately thoughts begin to go through his head, *I am a failure. I probably won't even graduate college. What will my parents think? I'll never be able to get a job and I'll be a bum the rest of my life. Then obviously I will never get married because what girl wants to marry a bum!* Jason feels upset and depressed. Not because of the situation but because of what he *thinks* about the situation. If he continues such thoughts over and over throughout the coming days and even weeks, this feeling of gloominess will linger.

Now imagine Steve, Jason's roommate. He receives similar grades but thinks, *Oh well, I didn't like that class anyway. My grades aren't as good as I wanted, but who says I have to have straight As? My parents will love me no matter what grade I get. When I go to get a job all they want is my diploma. An employer doesn't care what letter grade I got. I'm sure I'll do better next semester. After all, this was my first year. I have to give myself some slack.* Steve goes on to enjoy the rest of the night while Jason makes some excuse to retire early.

The same point can be made by using an example of two women who have been trying to get pregnant for several years. One is completely depressed because she is thinking, *Something must be wrong with my body. I'll never be able to have children. I am a failure as a woman. I am worthless if I can't be a mother.* She is depressed. The other woman still badly wants a child but entertains thoughts such as: *I have so much to offer children all around me. Sometimes it takes many years to have a baby; maybe my time hasn't come yet. Even if I never have children of my own, there is so much I can do with my life, like furthering my education, touring the world with my husband, serving others, or adopting. I know that God has a plan for me.* This woman is not depressed because she interprets the same exact situation in a true and more positive way. Plus, she doesn't waste away her life sulking; she accomplishes great things while she is waiting (on the Lord's time) for that blessing.

Many athletes meditate before they compete, and this positive imaging usually improves their game. People who think positively overall are generally healthier. The mind is a powerful thing.

13

My mother taught me the same concept several years ago when she explained the following story, which demonstrates anxious feelings. Say you are home alone at night, lying in bed, and you hear a scratching noise on the front door. Instantly your heart begins to race. Your palms become sweaty. You begin breathing faster. These are all physiological things. And why did they happen? Because of the noise?—no! Because of what you *thought* about the noise! You were probably thinking, *Oh no! What if someone is trying to break in?* In the same scenario if you owned a dog, then you would just blow it off thinking, *Oh, it's just the dog.* Then you would probably roll over and fall back asleep. Can you begin to see how what you think creates a *physical* change inside your body? Your *thoughts* can initiate the adrenaline rush, depressive mood, or happy response in your body.

Going through nursing school, I was fascinated with the mechanisms and chemicals that actually control our mood. Let's use my mother's example. Say you just heard the scratch on your front door. It's late at night and the thought *What if someone is trying to break in?* runs through your mind. A couple of things happen when you think this. Your sympathetic nervous system goes to work. It triggers your adrenal gland—more precisely the adrenal medulla—to secrete epinephrine and norepinephrine, catecholamines that contribute to the stress response in your body. These chemicals make the blood vessels in your skin and intestines constrict while dilating the vessels to the organs you need to function immediately, increasing the blood flow to the skeletal muscles and lungs; all of which contributes to an increased heart rate and blood pressure.[4] This systematic response gives your heart and lungs increased blood so that if a burglar really were at your door, you would have enough breath and oxygenated muscles to run as fast and far as you could or else you would have increased physical strength if you chose to stay and fight. That is why this response is often called *fight or flight*. Your breath is deepened and your palms are cool and sweaty because of the lack of blood flow to your fingers. If you were eating something at the time, your stomach would say, "Forget about me, you have more important things to worry about now." So your digestive process slows or possibly stops in order to better accommodate the essential organs, resulting in a dry mouth. Steroids are also released from the adrenal cortex, some of which are glucocorticoids. These steroids increase the body's blood sugar, giving you a burst of energy to run or fight. Blood flow is also increased in your brain, allowing for more mental alertness.[5] I know it's a mouthful, but I want you to understand the physical changes that take place inside your body in response to certain anxious or negative thoughts.

Have you ever been up on the stand waiting to give a speech, and you could tell that the speaker just ahead of you is starting to wrap it up? The thought *It's almost my turn* triggers your mouth to feel like it's full of cotton (digestive process slowing), your hands get all sweaty, and you can nearly hear your heart pounding in your chest. Any *perceivably frightening* thought can create this reaction. I imagine our Creator instilled this type of system in our bodies so that we could deal with emergencies. You bet you'd be able to run faster than normal if a tiger was right behind you because this stress response will give you as much help as it can to get you out of a dangerous situation. (The problem is we aren't in life or death situations often—only situations that we *perceive* to be upsetting). These chemical exchanges are associated with anxiety; however, just as your body crashes after you have lots of simple sugars, your body will also crash after steroid sugars and adrenaline rushes. This cycle of anxiety-producing thoughts will often lead to depression because your body can only run on adrenaline for so long before it runs out, leaving you weary and ultimately depressed.

Chronic anxiety leads to a more unhealthy life as well. Lewis, Heitkemper, and Dirksen say, "Stress has been identified to contribute to a wide range of diseases, including: cardiovascular disease, cancer, arthritis, multiple sclerosis, irritable bowel syndrome, fibromyalgia, colds, and asthma."[6]

Maybe you are beginning to panic—don't! It's okay. Don't let this information stress you out even more. You will learn to reduce your stressful anxious thoughts soon. Not only will learning to control your stress prevent many of these health problems from occurring, but, often, nagging health concerns you already have will clear up on their own once your anxiety is resolved.

Just as scary thoughts create an anxious response, negative thoughts can create a depressed response. Negative thoughts such as *I'm not a good mother, I'm not a good father, I am ugly, My job is worthless, I am weak, I am sad, I will never feel happy, My family would be better off without me* can also produce a physiological response. In the pathways of the neurological system, there are gaps called synapses. On one side of the gap there are sites that release chemicals throughout the day into the synapses. I am specifically referring to the cerebral cortex and limbic system in the brain, which deal primarily with emotion.[7]

Serotonin, dopamine, and norepinephrine are amine transmitters that studies suggest give you the "feel good" sense. A popular theory suggests that an increase or decrease of these three chemicals, within the neurological synapse, contribute to the emotions of depression.[8]

This hypothesis suggests that you experience the euphoric, or happy feelings, when these chemicals build up in the synapse and lock into their matching receptor on the other side of the gap. Keep in mind that these chemicals are also being reabsorbed—recycled in a sense—to maintain a balance within the synapse. This process acts similarly to a thermostat in your home, except it controls mood instead of temperature by increasing or decreasing these chemicals. Certain antidepressant medications such as Prozac, Zoloft, and Celexa are called SSRI's, or selective serotonin reuptake inhibitors, which is just a fancy way of saying that they inhibit serotonin from being reabsorbed (or recycled). That way more serotonin can stay in the synapse longer, resulting in more of them reaching their receptor sites, thus increasing your feelings of happiness.[9]

Antidepressants help many people who suffer from depression, but just remember, they only treat the symptom, not the disease. They won't make your depression go away, but they may help you feel better temporarily or at least give you that extra oomph to help you in your quest to retrain your thinking. I personally believe antidepressants improve mood partly because you think, *This pill will help me feel happy.* Your

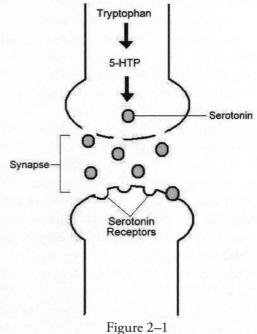

Figure 2–1

16

encouraging thought along with the medication itself provides therapeutic results. The true cure for most people is learning to give yourself the *right* chemical exchanges by thinking positively. But until you can master your thoughts, medication may be required. Figure 2–1 shows the synaptic process in the neurological system.

It is insightful to note that some illegal drugs work in this same manner. Cocaine has been known to create euphoric feelings by blocking dopamine from being reabsorbed in the synapse, thus escalating the amount of dopamine available to lock into the matching receptors.[10] These drugs, however, are harmful to the body and are extremely dangerous. People don't do drugs because they are bad people. They do drugs because they want to feel good. Using illegal drugs is definitely not the answer, but feeling happy is a desirable goal.

What I want you to take away from all of this is that . . . what you *think* affects your *mood*! Exactly how, exactly why, we don't know precisely, but there is a direct correlation between your thoughts and your mood. And now that you know this, you can begin the learning process to stop the negative, scary thoughts and learn to replace them with positive, happy thoughts, which can generate the sense of well-being in your life.

I believe some people suffer from depression while others may not because some personalities and situations may foster more negative thoughts than others. By nature, I am prone to negative thoughts. All people are given different trials. Some are easily drawn into alcohol abuse, some to gambling, some to gossiping, some to same gender attraction, some to negative thoughts. Just because some people were born with a gambling personality does not give them permission to waste away their life savings in a slot machine. Our personality flaws are not justification for wrongful actions. Negative thinking is no different. Don't use the excuse *I was just born this way. I can't help it.* Or *My parents raised me this way.* Rationalizing will not solve the problem, but hard work to change habitual behavior will. Every time we overcome one of our trials with dignity, we become more like God—more full of light, more able to combat the evil one. Remember: God can make our weak things become strong (Ether 12:27). But we must do our part.

Take Action:

- Recognize your symptoms of depression or anxiety. **Write** them down. Understanding how depression and anxiety are manifested in your life will help you recognize it quicker when it comes.

- Schedule a visit with your physician. It is important to rule out other health problems. Anxiety, in particular, has symptoms that coincide with other illnesses. For example, hyperthyroidism can cause you to experience nervousness, palpitations, and shortness of breath.

NOTES

1. Demitri Papolos, MD, and Janice Demitri, MD, *Overcoming Depression: The Definitive Resource for Patients and Families Who Live with Depression and Manic-Depression* (New York, NY: HarperCollins Publishers, 1997), 8.

2. Edmund J. Bourne, PhD, *The Anxiety and Phobia Workbook* (Oakland, California: New Harbinger Publications, 2010), 5–6.

3. David D. Burns, M.D., *Feeling Good: The New Mood Therapy.* (New York, NY: William Morrow and Company, 1999), 12.

4. Sharon M. Lewis, RN, PhD, FAAN, et all., *Medical-Surgical Nursing: Assessment and Management of Clinical Problems: Sixth edition* (St. Louis, Missouri: Mosby, 2004), 118, figure 8.5.

5. Ibid., 118, figure 8.5; 119.

6. Ibid., 121.

7. Ibid., 118.

8. Burns, *Feeling Good: The New Mood Therapy*, 436.

9. Ibid., 433–39.

10. Lewis, *Medical-Surgical Nursing*, 176.

Chapter Three

SELF-MASTERY—"BE YE THEREFORE PERFECT"

From an early age, we are taught that the primary purpose of our earthly existence is to obtain a physical body and to be tried and tested. In essence, we are here to become like God—to learn how to put off the natural man (Mosiah 3:19) and to practice self-mastery. Overcoming a weakness of humanity, such as depression, is an amazing feat. It requires the soul to be stronger than the mind. When the brain thinks negatively, it becomes the soul's greatest task to push this natural man away and allow the light of Christ to fill our entire being. It requires total self-control.

During my first year in college, my mother shared with me a program she had recently come across. It taught me some skills to overcome depression. Instead of masking the symptoms with medication, I began the difficult process of "mastering" my thoughts. As I noticed remarkable improvement in my mood, I began searching for more cognitive therapies. I loved the idea that I had the control to determine how I felt simply by thinking in a healthier way. I realized that the concepts I learned had similarities to gospel principles. This scriptural support made them even more legitimate in my mind.

As I discuss methods to overcome depression, I feel it is important to include the scriptures because the holy pages are like a treasure chest containing precious gems of life's greatest truths and answers to our daily predicaments. Simply reading and pondering the scriptures is the key to the chest. Within the pages, we learn powerful things. For the Spirit will tell us and even show us *all* things that we should do

(2 Nephi 32:3–5). I believe this includes how to be happy. Psalms 119:105 says, "Thy word is a lamp unto my feet, and a light unto my path." The word—meaning the scriptures—will light our path and show us the way; the way to happiness.

CONTROL YOUR THOUGHTS

"When your life is complete in mortality, it will be the sum of your thoughts. That one suggestion has been a great blessing to me all my life, and it has enabled me upon many occasions to avoid thinking improperly because I realize that I will be, when my life's labor is complete, the product of my thoughts."[1]

—George Albert Smith

Practice makes perfect. This is especially pertinent when it comes to breaking the habit of negative thinking. If our goal in this life is to become more like God, then we must practice every day until we get it right. Just by living in this world, we are given daily opportunities to practice. I imagine we will never meet the goal of perfection in this lifetime, but we are encouraged to try and improve ourselves while in this life (Alma 34:33). In this section, you will learn how to practice controlling your thoughts, which will promote greater happiness.

Satan, the great liar, would have you believe many negative and incorrect things about yourself. Herein lies the battle of controlling your thoughts. Right now I am not talking about dirty or inappropriate thoughts but rather thoughts that are discouraging. Such as: *I'll never be good enough. I'll never be pretty or handsome enough. I'll never be good enough for God to accept me.* If you want to be happy, you must not entertain thoughts such as these; however, it is easier said than done.

In the *Ensign*, Jennifer Nuckols in her article entitled, "Truth and Lies," records the following, "Some of the greatest battles in my life haven't been literal battles but struggles in my own heart and mind against feelings of self-doubt, hopelessness, and fear. President Ezra Taft Benson (1899–1994) taught that this would be the case in the latter days: 'Satan is increasingly striving to overcome the Saints with despair, discouragement, despondency, and depression.' One way that Satan attempts to overcome us with such feelings is by telling us lies about our worth and about God's feelings toward us. . . . To combat such false beliefs that have negatively affected my attitudes and actions,

I have tried to consciously identify my own damaging thoughts and replace them with gospel truths." She goes on to explain that Satan would even have us misinterpret scripture or whatever it takes to make us believe that we are not loved by our Father in Heaven.[2]

Once you recognize how destructive your negative thoughts and Satan's lies can be to your mental health, you must stop them. However, it is nearly impossible to tell yourself to merely stop thinking a certain way. You have probably been a negative thinker a good portion of your life. This is not an easy habit to break. It is not good enough to say, *Okay, I will ignore Satan and think more positively.* It won't work. When depression strikes, it is usually because of repetitive negative thoughts that we allow to stay in our mind. Many counselors recommend the following exercise as a tool to help you take control of your thoughts. It is an indispensable step you must take to actually break the habit of negative thinking.

First, go grab a notebook, or use the provided form at the back of the book. If you are using your own paper, draw a line down the middle of the page to make two columns. Next you must actually write out all of your negative thoughts that you have throughout the day. Write the negative thought on the left column and then write down a positive and true replacement statement in the right column. This sounds easy, but it takes time. Synthesizing your thoughts into an actual sentence is difficult. Many people subconsciously think negatively. You will have to thoroughly examine all thoughts you have, extract the actual sentence you think, and transpose it to paper. It is important that you actually write them down, not just envision them. Once you do this for so long, you may be able to skip the writing it out part, and your mind will do it automatically. But until it becomes automatic, write your thoughts down.

For example, you might have thoughts like this come to mind: *I don't want to go to work today! It is so boring there. I can't stand to do this every single day!* Thoughts like this, if they are continually repeated in your mind day after day, will make you depressed. Write it down in your notebook, and to the side of it write a positive and true statement such as: *I am a free person. I can get a different job if I want to. Even the best job in the world has boring or unpleasant parts to it. I am providing for my family and making a difference in the world.* It is important to be realistic when correcting your thoughts, otherwise you won't believe yourself. So you wouldn't say, *I love my job. I will have a good day today because I have a great job!* If you don't love your job, this statement is useless. If you truly want to start attacking your depression head on, I challenge you to diligently stick to this exercise. It may get tiresome because you must write down every single negative thought. You'll probably fill up an entire notebook, but you will notice a difference in the end. Eventually you will make the switch from negative to positive automatically. Do this exercise as long as it takes to train your brain to think positively. You'll know you are through when days go by and you seldom have a negative thought to write down.

The difficulty lies in trying to come up with those positive statements. It definitely takes practice, but it gets easier. If it helps, try imagining what a friend or your mother would say to you after you divulged a negative thought. For example, if you wrote down, "That was the worst talk I have ever given in church. I made so many mistakes. I'm sure everyone at church thinks I'm dumb now!" Think about what a friend would say if you shared this thought out loud. They would probably tell you, "Hey, you did a great job! Most people were too busy stuffing Cheerios in their kid's mouth to even notice the one little goof-up you made. Plus, you are the only one who knew what you planned to say, so no one noticed that you said something wrong." If imagining a friend or mother doesn't work, then go grab an actual friend or family member to help you come up with an alternate statement.

The more you do this exercise, the more you will notice how irrational and false your negative thoughts are. When you're stuck in depression, your thinking becomes distorted and you begin telling yourself things that aren't even true. While depressed, you honestly feel as if everything in your past was terribly sad and that your future holds nothing but suffering as well.[3] You start to believe these ridiculous thoughts. "It seems real because it *feels* real."[4] Once you read your thoughts on paper, it should become more obvious that you have been deceiving yourself. Take the example in the previous paragraph. *That was the worst talk I have ever given.* Well, I'm sure you gave a talk or two as a child where you stumbled on your words or even had a parent whisper the words into your ear. Surely that was worse. Or how about, *I'm sure everyone at church thinks I'm dumb now!* First of all, not everyone can think you're dumb. Is it logical that every single person at church thinks you're dumb? No way! Maybe one or two, but everyone?—that's ridiculous. Using words like *always*, *never*, *everyone*, and *no one* seldom apply and are signs of irrational thinking. For some reason we think in black or white; it's all or nothing. But this is not a healthy thinking pattern. Just remember that training your brain to think differently takes time, so be patient with yourself.

When I first took on the challenge of writing out my thoughts, I was having serious doubts about the profession I chose. I was overwhelmed by the nursing program that I had just started, so I was having some anxious thoughts. Also, I was seriously dating the man who is now my husband. Though I wanted to marry him, the weight of such an important decision added to my anxiety. This is an actual excerpt from my personal notebook.

Negative Thoughts	Positive Replacement Thoughts
What if I get my degree and I hate being a nurse? I don't want to be miserable my whole life.	I love to be around people. I am young. If I don't like being a nurse, I have time to do something else afterward. Nursing is very diversified—I have many options once I get my degree. Even if I never practice as a nurse, this information will bless the lives of my future family.
Once I'm a nurse, what if I make a horrible error or kill someone?	Nurses aren't required to have perfect knowledge. I can always look things up in medical books. There is no such thing as a perfect nurse. Most errors are simple anyway and can be easily corrected. I won't kill anyone.
What if I don't pass the program?	I have always gotten good grades before. Nothing will change. I have always been good at science-related subjects. I will pass.
What if I marry the wrong person?	I am living worthy of the Spirit to guide my life. I have received a "Yes" answer. Heavenly Father would warn me through the Holy Ghost if he was wrong for me. Have faith. Trust God.
What if I feel depressed for the rest of my life?	I have gotten through this before, I can do it again. I have the skills to change my thoughts now. I have support from family and friends. The Lord will help me overcome it.

I had many thoughts, but these were some of the recurring ones. So I reread my notebook many times a day. Some days I had to read them many times each hour. Once in awhile, I would add a new scary thought I had or a new negative thought that came to my mind and then write out a positive replacement thought to the side of it. Each time I read the right column of my notebook, a sense of peace came over me. I felt reassured, and my depression would lessen. After a month or two of doing this every single day, I found myself doing it automatically by making the correction in my head. Once a negative thought came in my mind, I would talk myself right out of it. Even more amazing—eventually, the negative thoughts hardly ever came around. The majority of my thoughts became empowering and positive. As a result, my depression ceased! My positive replacement thoughts weren't just something to make me feel better. They were true! Today I have found a slice of nursing I enjoy. I did pass my program and boards and I'm still madly in love with my husband. Why entertain thoughts that aren't even true?

The following chart shows examples of more negative thoughts with positive replacements.[5]

Negative Thoughts	Positive Replacement Thoughts
I never do anything right!	Sometimes I make mistakes, but I am human. And humans make mistakes. I do a lot of things right.
I just yelled at my son again. I am such a bad parent! My son would be better off without me.	Again, I am human. I can't be perfect right now. I can only work on getting better each day. Obviously my son would be worse off without me. I feed him, clothe him, and keep him safe. I can show increased love to him now and he will know I love him.
I am so stupid!	I am not stupid. Maybe I did a stupid thing, but I'm only human.
She probably thinks I'm such a goof! (after fumbling my words while conversing)	So what if I fumbled my words. I can't read minds. I have no idea what she thinks about me. Maybe she thought it was funny or maybe it comforted her that I fumbled my words because she does it sometimes too.

I'm late for my meeting! Everyone will think I'm a slacker. My boss will be disappointed in me.	It is not possible that every single person will think poorly of me. Maybe some will feel bad wondering if I had trouble on my way to work. Even if my boss is disappointed, it's not like I'm late every day. If he/she doesn't understand, then they are unrealistic about the fact that everyone makes mistakes. I can do better to plan ahead next time, or plan to be early if being late means losing my job.
It's my fault that my child has rejected the gospel. I should have been a better parent.	Even some of Lehi's children were disobedient to God's commandments and he was a pretty good parent. My children have their agency. I did the best I could with the knowledge I had at the time.
What if my husband wrecks on his way home from work?	Worrying won't change anything. The route home from work has low speed limits, so even if he were to wreck on his way home, it would probably just be a fender bender.

Bruce K. Fordham, in an article titled, "Think About What you are Thinking About," wrote the following:

> When the human brain is introduced to any new activity, it begins to build a new pathway. The more often the activity is repeated, the more solid and automatic that pathway becomes. An analogy might further explain this concept: You are standing at the edge of the jungle and know that you must find a way through it. You notice that a path, well worn and easy to travel, has already been cut through the undergrowth for you. But then you notice signs warning of dangers lurking at the end of the path, and even though it appears to be the easiest route, you determine that it might be best to forge your own path. You pull out a machete and start hacking through the thick growth and underbrush. It's tough work! When you glance up and again notice the path that has already been cut, you become discouraged. But you persevere, eventually carving out your own path. You use it frequently as you traverse the jungle, and in time it becomes the obvious, preferred path. Meanwhile, the original well-worn path—the one with danger at the end—deteriorates from lack of use.
>
> The jungle, of course, represents our brains; the initial well-worn

path is the route of our undesirable thoughts. The new path represents our efforts to forge new and righteous thoughts, habits, and behaviors.[6]

The more we think positive true statements about ourselves and others, the more comfortable and automatic they will be. They will come as freely and naturally as did our old thinking pattern—the negative way. Even if we have a weak moment or a hard trial and fall back into our old pattern of negative thinking, we will at least be more conscious of our mistake and will be able to get back on the track of positive thinking quicker than before.

Let me make it clear that the first few weeks or even months of this thought-changing process requires serious hard work. You might get a couple of days into it and look back only to realize you've only cleared about three feet of your "mental jungle" with miles to go until you make it through. You will feel discouraged thinking it is impossible that positive thoughts will ever come naturally to you. Stop—write that thought down, replace it with a correct and positive statement, then pick up that machete and persevere. The beginning is obviously the hardest, but once the initial new path has been established, each time you travel through it, it becomes smoother. The undergrowth becomes trampled and, day by day, month by month, the old path—the one you thought you'd never leave—is becoming less obvious to discern as vegetation overcomes it.

Between the two small towns of Delta, Utah, and Oak City, Utah, there are two roads. One is a nicely paved road that has only been there for twenty years. Most of my generation is unaware that another road between the two towns even existed. The original road probably began as most roads do. A group of people needed to get from point A to point B, and they needed to get there on a regular basis. Where the travelers would go, plant life would die, rocks were dislodged from their place, and over time an obvious path became visible. Eventually there were so many traveling this path, someone decided to pave it and it became a road. This road, however, followed the natural curvature of the land and wasn't the most time-efficient route. Many years later, someone decided to create a new road between the towns—one that was more direct to save traveling time (Figure 3–2). With the new road completed, cars began traveling down it instead of the old one. As you can see from the photograph (Figure 3–1), twenty years of being unused has made this road somewhat difficult to discern. Sand has blown over it; weeds have grown through the cracks. Only those who knew it was there can even pick out its location. Possibly another twenty years from now, this road will not be visible at all.

Figure 3–1

Figure 3–2

The battle between positive and negative thinking in our minds is much like the contrast between these two roads. With time and effort, we form new pathways of positive thinking in our minds as we quit using the pathways of negative thoughts. In time, those pathways become less and less visible and eventually fade and disappear.

What then is the factor that establishes the jungle path or the well-paved road? It is use. Consistently using the same route overtime will establish the path you will have in your mind—the one that is natural—that you go down without even realizing. Consistent negativity breeds a negative path. Consistent positivity breeds a positive path.

A quote from Dr. Jill Ammon-Wexler, doctor of psychology and brain researcher, explains how changing your thoughts can actually change the physical connections in the brain.

> You have about 30 billion neurons—the nerve cells responsible for conducting information throughout your brain. And if you were to stretch those tiny neurons end to end, they would actually stretch about 6000 miles. This is approximately the distance from the surface of the Earth to the moon and back, and it is all packed into the 3+ pounds of your physical brain . . . All of your beliefs, your habits, everything making up your mental reality, is contained in physical neural pathways. Each time you think a thought, it is communicated among your neurons via tiny electro-chemical messages. The first time you have an experience or learn something new, chances are a new pathway is created. Then the next time you have that experience, your brain will search to see if you have experienced it before. If you have, it will follow the same pathway. The more often you have that experience or think that thought, the most physically complex and durable the neural pathway holding that thought will become. This is how a thought or action becomes a habit. . . . You cannot rationally "think" these physical networks away. That's why it is so hard to break a habit. Your habit is wired into your brain as actual physical connections. . . . Two things create strong neural pathways: Repetition, and intense emotion. So the basic secret of change is this: (1) Stir up and allow yourself to truly "feel" intense negative emotion about what you wish to change, (2) Select an alternate positive behavior or thought pattern, (3) Associate your new pattern with even stronger positive emotion, (4) Reward yourself with praise each time you replace the old pattern with the new one, and (5) Make it a point to repeat this as often as possible.[7]

So though it may be difficult, within yourself you hold the power to create new pathways. The machete is in your hand, and I know you can do it. Begin by making the commitment that you will give this exercise a whole-hearted effort. It may be beneficial to have someone support you through it by continually reminding you to write down your thoughts or at least follow up with you to make sure you did it. A common negative thought one might have is, *This exercise seems pretty lame. I bet it won't help me.* Because of this thought, some don't even try it or if they begin, they give up after a few days. If given a chance, using this principle of "what you use, do, say, or think *most* becomes second nature," you will find empowerment to overcome more than just discouragement. You can overcome negativity, anxiety, addictions, and nearly any bad habit by creating new and better pathways. Old habits will slowly disappear as the foliage fills in the cracks from underuse. Your mind can change your life, and combined with the healing power of the Atonement, you can overcome anything!

Along with the thought-writing exercise, I use another method to fight negative thoughts. I like to fill my surroundings with wholesome things to read. I have a quote on my bathroom mirror that says, "We are troubled on every side, yet not distressed; we are perplexed, but not in despair; persecuted, but not forsaken; cast down, but not destroyed" (2 Corinthians 4:8–9). This scripture empowers me. I feel renewed energy to stand strong each time I read it. I have it in a place that I see every day because I tend to forget so quickly. It becomes much easier to rid our minds of negative thoughts when we are constantly filling them with strong wholesome thoughts. Here is another quote I love: "God didn't promise days without pain, laughter without sorrow, sun without rain, but He did promise strength for the day, comfort for the tears, and *light* for the way. —Author anonymous." So read good books. Listen to uplifting music. Read quotes or scriptures that fill you with hope.

In the Book of Mormon, King Benjamin taught the importance of controlling your thoughts when he said, "But this much I can tell you, that if ye do not watch yourselves, and your *thoughts*, and your words, and your deeds, and observe the commandments of God, and continue in the faith of what ye have heard concerning the coming of our Lord, even unto the end of your lives, ye must perish. And now, O man, remember, and perish not" (Mosiah 4:30, emphasis added).

As mentioned before, Satan uses thoughts in many different ways to tempt the children of God. We have all been told, "If you have a dirty thought, get rid of it immediately." I would like this to include negative thoughts. In the book of John we read, "This then is the message which we have heard of him, and declare unto you, that God is light, and in him is no darkness at all" (1 John 1:5). The more we are able to control our thoughts and actions, the more we become like God; and the more happy we become.

You might be thinking, *This "change your thought" stuff might work if you had a happy life, but what about me? My life really is depressing!* True, there is no magic pill to take away all your sadness, but changing your thoughts still improves your mood and functionality.

My uncle, who is a truck driver, experienced a huge tragedy several years ago. While taking a load to California in his semi, he received a phone call informing him that his wife and four daughters were in a horrible accident on the freeway where they had rolled their SUV. He was told his oldest daughter had been killed instantly and his wife had passed away in the back of the ambulance en route to the hospital. He was six hours away from the hospital where his three remaining daughters were recovering. He was advised to park his semi and wait for someone to come and drive him to the hospital. He remained calm and insisted he was able to drive himself. He arrived safely, which is amazing because I can only imagine how devastated he would be after such a call. Luckily my uncle had prepared his testimony for such a trial. His faith and positive attitude continue to help him raise his three remaining daughters and to press on each day.

Even in the face of extremely difficult trials, our thoughts can still determine our overall mood. Imagine if my uncle thought: *My life is over. I will never be happy again. I can't do this. Why has God done this to me?* These are negative, even false statements. I visited with my uncle and he told me these were his thoughts, "I have always known that life would send hard things my way. I never expected to sail through life without something bad happening. I felt like nothing very hard had happened to me yet and I was due for something to test me. I think when God lets you go through something like I have been through, it is, in a way, a compliment that He knows you can make it okay. I can do anything with the Lord's help. I know this is hard, but the sadness will lessen with time and I will be happy again. Other people have gone through tragedies, and I have seen them smile again. I will be okay—the Lord will help me." My uncle is an amazing man and a great example to me of someone who "lives in the light." I can see by what he said that it is because of his firm testimony in Christ and his upbeat attitude that he was able to get through the funeral and lonely times without falling apart. He knows the Lord is guiding and comforting him. I have watched in amazement as the Lord has done just that.

Take Action:

- Control your thoughts. In sentence form, write down your negative thoughts and replace them with true and positive thoughts. Do this exercise for as long as it takes to retrain your brain to think positively. Learning to recognize and rewrite negative thinking may require support from a professional.

- Pray. The Spirit can teach you what things you should be thinking about yourself. He can help you recognize and replace your negative thoughts. Listen to your prayers. Do they sound negative just like your thoughts? Try to use positive phrases while conversing with your Father in Heaven.

SELF-EXPECTATIONS—THE "I SHOULD" PROBLEM

To a great extent, expectations are what drive us to be the productive perfectionist people that we are. Often people with depression have unrealistic expectations. Then when that expectation is not met (because it was basically impossible), the person is left feeling worthless and disheartened. What is it about us that causes us to think we can do everything—and do it all perfectly? I know at least from a woman's perspective we feel that we should be wonderful wives and mothers, terrific cooks, perfect housekeepers, honorable church members, 100-percent visiting teachers, PTA stars, soccer cheerleaders, and stay fit as a fiddle after having several children. We expect such great things out of ourselves that often cannot be achieved simultaneously or even at all. Why is just trying our best not enough? Who says we *should* be all these things? Yes, As Christians we are expected to work toward these goals. But don't forget—It is through Christ's Atonement that we can reach this station in life. But we forget that it is through Christ's Atonement that we can reach this station in life. We do all we can and He makes up the rest. It is easy to forget this when our minds get congested with piles of life's expectations.

A key element in mastering your cognitions is having realistic expectations about yourself and about the people and events that surround you. We are always telling ourselves "I should" statements. For example, we may think: *I should lose weight. I should be happy. I should be a better wife/husband/parent/son/daughter. I should make more money.* And the list goes on and on. To all of those statements we should say back, *Who says I should?* We tend to place rigid expectations on ourselves. We believe we are only of worth if we achieve these self-imposed "should" statements, never minding, of course, the source of the preposterous expectation. For example, once I was visiting with a friend when I heard her say, "I should have lost my baby weight by now." I asked why. "Well, because it's been a year since Katy was born," she replied. "So what?" I said. "Who says the baby weight has to be off in one year?" She thought about this for a moment and then told me that no one told her that, she just expected herself to lose weight quickly after the baby was born because her sisters all did. She came from a fairly thin family and being around them made her feel self-conscious.

We may view other people and gauge ourselves by that standard. Why? Once you chain yourself to an unrealistic "I should" statement, you have set yourself up for failure. Consider the source of your "I should" statements. My friend had unwisely set a standard for her weight according to what her family members weighed or what seemingly beautiful women on TV weighed. Never mind that after years of research, scientist's have come up with charts and measurements to determine healthy weight—of which her weight fell within the normal range. She was not happy or satisfied, however, because the source of her expectation was unreliable.

Who says you should make more money? Who says you should dust the house once a week? Who says you should be a better mother? What is a perfect mother anyway? Who says you should be crafty? Who says you should take freshly baked cookies to every neighbor you ever have? As far as I'm concerned, there is no specific body type one should have. There is no set amount that is an acceptable salary. There is no definite grieving time after the loss of a loved one. There is no written list of what a good mother is and what she is not. As you begin recognizing your "I should" statements, please also ask yourself where the source of that expectation is coming from.

What about the statement, "I should lose weight"? Now if losing weight is important to *you*, then go ahead and work on it. But if losing weight is just something the world says is important, get rid of that thought. Don't let these guilt-streaked statements suffocate you. Replacing those negative "I should" statements is imperative. The "shoulds" that are important to you will become much more achievable if you aren't continually beating yourself down, but instead using positive and uplifting thoughts to motivate yourself. Set reasonable goals and praise yourself for even the smallest successes.

One time in college, I became particularly bogged down. I had more homework than I anticipated and my job was demanding too much of my time. My grades were starting to suffer and my depression seemed to escalate. Cutting back on school was not something I could do, so the job was my only option. I kept telling myself, *You should be able to do this. You should be able to handle a job and school; everyone else does.* Furthermore, I was afraid my boss would think I was weak if I asked him to cut back on my hours. The stress of worrying what to do intensified my depression. I wasn't able to take care of myself and each time I went to work, I got that familiar knot in my stomach. Finally one night while reading my scriptures, the following words in 2 Nephi 8 spoke straight to my heart: "Hearken unto me, ye that know righteousness, the people in whose heart I have written my law, fear ye not the reproach of men, neither be ye afraid of their revilings. . . . I am he; yea, I am he that comforteth you. Behold, who art thou, that thou shouldst be afraid of man, who shall die, and of the son of man, who shall be made like unto grass" (2 Nephi 8:7 & 12). And the end of verse eleven reads, "and they shall obtain gladness and joy; *sorrow and mourning shall flee away*" (emphasis added). That day I realized an important truth, which I had heard before, but didn't process until that very moment. I learned that the only person I needed to please was God. If he was satisfied with me, then it didn't really matter what my boss thought, or anyone else for that matter. By being obedient to this principle I became much happier.

So when you think, *I should_____* (you fill in the blank), just evaluate it and if God says you should or if it is a "should" that is truly important to you, keep it. Throw the rest away. I'm quite positive God does not rate you on whether you are crafty or if your house is as clean as your neighbors. "The Lord is my light and my salvation; whom shall I fear? The Lord is the strength of my life; of whom shall I be afraid?" (Psalm 27:1). To me that says it so beautifully, but to make this even

LIVING IN THE LIGHT

more clear, ask yourself if the whisperings of the Holy Spirit are present with the "I should" statement. Look at the following list of "shoulds."

Examples of bad "shoulds"

- I should be able to resist this candy bar!—I'm such a weak person.
- I should be able to climb this hill without getting winded—I am so out of shape.
- I should know what I want to do with my life. Everyone else my age does.
- I should be able to get straight As.
- I should be a better housekeeper.
- I should be a better provider.
- I should be able to be happy on my own without having to take a pill for it.

In contrast with . . .

Examples of possible promptings

- I should call that girl in my ward. She looked lonely on Sunday.
- I should stop and help that person pick up the books they just dropped in the school hall.
- I should leave this party. Something doesn't feel right about being here.
- I should read this quote in my lesson next Sunday. I don't know why but maybe someone needs it.
- I should stop by and visit _____ (you fill in the blank).

Can you determine the difference between the two kinds of "shoulds"? Understanding and recognizing the feelings of the Holy Ghost will help you resolve which shoulds to act upon and which shoulds to discard. In Moroni 7:13 we read: "But behold, that which is of God inviteth and enticeth to do good continually; wherefore, every-thing which inviteth and enticeth to do good, and to love God, and to serve him, is inspired of God."

Often there are ways to simplify a task that you really *do* want to complete, making it more achievable. For example, if you really would like to have dinner on the table when your husband gets home from work, increase your use of Crock-Pot meals so the children have your attention in the late afternoon when they are tired and need you most. Or make cookies in sessions, throwing the dough in the fridge when the kids get fussy and finish baking them the next day. Buy a dessert from the store to take to your child's school party instead of spending hours decorating homemade cupcakes.

A husband who truly feels he "should" exercise but also knows he "should" spend time with his family can try doing both at the same time. Forego the gym membership and play soccer with your kids on the back lawn or go for a family bike ride.

A college student who desires to work while also striving for better grades might seek employment where they can study on the job. Healthy meals can be time-consuming to prepare, so weight loss might become more realistic if one purchases instant brown rice, prewashed and cut fruits and vegetables, and precooked diced chicken, and so on. This compromise might mean spending a little more at the grocery store, but if it is a "should" you truly wish for, the extra money is money well spent.

Take a moment now to write out a list of your "shoulds." Cross off the ones that you need to get rid of. You may have to redo this exercise occasionally as new shoulds come into your life. Don't be afraid to write down the good shoulds on a different piece of paper when they occasionally come to mind. Doing so will increase the likelihood of acting upon the prompting.

Take Action:

- **Develop realistic expectations of yourself.** Write a list of all your "shoulds." With each "should," ask yourself, "Is this realistic? Is it helpful? Would I place this expectation on a spouse, child, or friend?" If the answer is no, then cross it off and let it go from your life. If it is a prompting from the Spirit, do your best to accomplish it.

EXPECTATIONS OF OTHERS AND EVENTS

In the Book of Mormon, Mosiah teaches, "And see that all these things are done in wisdom and order; for it is not requisite that a man should run faster than he has strength. And again, it is expedient that he should be diligent, that thereby he might win the prize; therefore, all things must be done in order" (Mosiah 4:27). Although the bar is raised for us as Christians, even our Father in Heaven only requires that we are *diligent* throughout our lives in order to obtain the prize, which is eternal life. Is there a reason we ask more from ourselves than He does? Pray to find a balance. Pray to find order. When you feel dark or down, ask yourself what thought you just allowed your mind to dwell on. Was it an unrealistic expectation you put on yourself or an inappropriate "should"? If so, chances are they are contributing to your feeling blue.

I used to wake up in the morning and mentally plan out my day. A typical "to do" list might include:

To Do:

- Exercise for thirty minutes
- Scriptures and prayer
- Laundry
- Vacuum
- Wash dishes
- Grocery shop
- Set up visiting teaching
- Read to kids
- Work on Sunday School lesson
- Practice shapes and colors with my toddler
- Make something wonderful and completely homemade for dinner

But the day usually went like this:

- Baby alarm goes off. (My alarm clock is special. Not only does it wake me up in the morning, it wakes me at least three different times in the night as well.)
- Exercised five minutes—stopped to replace the pacifier back in the mouth of the screaming baby. Exercised five more minutes—stopped to catch toddler from escaping out front door. Exercised five more minutes—stopped to take toddler to the bathroom. Turned off exercise video with a sigh.
- Burnt the toast. Fire alarm goes off—woke the baby from his nap.
- Began reading scriptures. Two verses completed before page is

torn out by toddler. Said a prayer for strength not to kill her.

- Showered, rushed off to the store. Left my wallet home so I had to go back and get it.
- Back from the store—read books to my kids before their nap.
- Threw in a load of laundry.
- An old friend called just as I began working on my lesson so I chatted instead.
- Tried to clean up the house, but my toddler messed it up faster than I could clean.
- No time for an amazing dinner so the family got spaghetti . . . again.
- My husband comes home from work and I spend at least five minutes trying to persuade him that I really didn't sit on my bottom all day watching soap operas, even though the house looks like a bomb went off. My little one gets a fever so I'm up half the night with him thinking to myself: *I didn't accomplish anything today! And I only have two kids! What do people with six do?* And to make matters worse I realize that I forgot to change the clothes over to the dryer!

So I used to feel depressed much of the time thinking that my days were worthless, or my vacations were never good enough, or holidays were never as wonderful as I imagined. The problem is that we live in an imperfect world and yet expect to live perfect lives and have perfect children, vacations, holidays, and even days where we get everything done that we want. We don't need to lower our expectations but perhaps make them more realistic. I still have a list of things I wish to accomplish each day, but I say to myself each morning: *This is what I hope happens, but I'm going to have a great day no matter what comes my way.* And now my morning prayers always include *What do you want me to accomplish today?* Then when I'm sitting in the rocking chair at the end of the day, holding my sick child, I realize that the day was more productive than I thought. I kept my children alive! I somehow managed to have some laundry done in the previous days because I am wearing clothes, and my family is full from the dinner I made. I improved my relationship with a friend (which surely is more important than vacuuming!), and I am holding the most precious little boy in the world and soaking up every second of it.

We don't need to grumble about rained-out vacations either. We can think, *Oh well, I guess we can't go to the beach as we planned, so let's go to the museum instead.* Instead of feeling depressed around the holidays because it didn't snow, you burnt the ham, and your spouse didn't get you the gift you heavily hinted about, you can think, *I am surrounded by loving family and I have the opportunity to celebrate the birth of Christ. That's all that really matters.* Do bad things happen to people in the world? (you should be thinking . . . *yes*) And are you a person? (*Yes.*) Then just expect that you might get a flat tire, you might have a handicapped child, you might burn a few dinners, you might lose a loved one to cancer, or you might gain a few pounds because it just plain isn't reasonable to believe that life will always be perfect. If you have a mind-set to understand that hard things may come your way, you will not be as depressed and discouraged when they do. My father always says, "Hope for the best, but plan for the worst." Set realistic expectations for yourself, and you'll find you will meet them! Then feelings of triviality will blossom into feelings of self-satisfaction.

So you will probably be disappointed if you think your newborn will sleep through the night. A realistic expectation is to suppose he might get up five times and so when he only gets up twice, you are overjoyed! If you assume you will get a promotion at work and you don't, you will be discouraged with yourself. On the other hand, if you expect work to go on as normal, then you'll be tickled with the raise you get from your boss. If you anticipate being number one in your class, then that A- will bring you to tears. However, if you give your best efforts to your studies with full knowledge that you don't have to compete with anyone, your excellent GPA, perfect or not, will bring you self-assurance.

Young girls might be disappointed if they expect true love to take place as depicted in the fairy tale, Cinderella. Tell me, is this realistic? You go to the dance and meet a handsome guy who doesn't even bother to ask your name. Then, if you have a cute dainty foot you get to live happily ever after. Yeah right! I love a good fairy tale, and imaginative play is good for children. But take opportunities to teach your children how to think realistically. It is important for them to be able to discern between media and the real world.

You may want to take a moment to examine what expectations you have placed on your own family members. Are you expecting impossible things from them as well as from yourself? Are you expecting too much from your children and spouses and then letting them know that you are disappointed? Ellen Kreidman, PhD, says, we love a pet or a newborn baby simply because they are ours. We don't expect a new baby to help do the dishes, clean up their room, or perform certain tasks. We love them even though they do nothing for us in return. Somehow, when these babies grow up to be children and even older, we begin placing boundaries on our love. We say or think, *I'll love you if you get good grades. I'll love you if you make the baseball team.* We do the same to our spouses. *I'll love you if you make enough money. I'll love you if you pick up your dirty socks off the floor.* We can make our own family depressed by placing unrealistic expectations on them. Your relationship with them will improve if they know you love them simply because they belong to you. Not because of anything they do or don't do.[8]

Our Father in Heaven loves *you* perfectly. He loves you just because you're His child. Your worth to him is not dependent upon your occupation or social status. The expectations He places on you are achievable. He merely asks that we are diligent to the end, and that we love Him and our fellow men. He asks that we do all we can and allow Christ's Atonement to cover the rest. For we know it is by grace we are saved after all we can do (2 Nephi 25:23).

Take Action:

- **Develop realistic expectations of other people and events.** For example, before a vacation write down what you anticipate happening there. Or write down what you foresee happening on your first day at a new job. Even write down expectations you've placed on family members. Analyze which expectations are unrealistic or unimportant, and cross them off.

- **Practice anticipating events realistically.** Look forward to something and realize it may not happen as you planned. Think of ways to make it okay anyway.

- **Have a positive attitude.** Start every day off with a positive purpose or goal. At the end of each day you can feel regret over the ten things you *didn't* accomplish, or you can feel success for the one thing you *did*. It's all a matter of perspective.

NUTRITION, EXERCISE, AND ENDORPHINS

One aspect that nearly all professionals agree on is the importance of implementing a healthy lifestyle to improve your mental health. Eating more fresh fruits, vegetables, legumes, and complex carbohydrates, while decreasing the intake of simple sugars and caffeine, will help enhance your mood.

The Word of Wisdom, found in the Doctrine and Covenants, basically tells us the same thing. God's commandments truly are for our benefit. They are laws that lift, not the opposite. Verse nine in section 89 of the Doctrine and Covenants tells us to avoid hot drinks, which have been clarified to mean coffee and teas (Doctrine and Covenants 89:9). Caffeine acts as a stimulant, which increases your metabolism and energy, but only for a short time before you crash. Heavy caffeine users put themselves in a cycle of depression by ingesting the caffeine to wake them up. Then they stay up late with endless energy. By morning time, they have crashed, so they need more caffeine to stay awake.

In the same section in the Doctrine and Covenants, we are told to eat meat sparingly, and to eat whole grains, fruits, and vegetables (Doctrine and Covenants 89:12–15). Following these simple rules of self-care will increase your energy and give you the vigor to live a joyful productive life.

Avoiding junk food and empty calorie foods such as candy, white bread, donuts, and soda pop can help to circumvent depression. Simple sugars in the body act as quick energy; however, like caffeine they have a short life and leave you feeling down after the sugar has worn off. Also, sugar acts similarly to adrenaline, which is the catecholamine that makes you feel anxious. It functions as the glucocorticoids, which increase your blood sugar to provide energy for you to run away from that tiger. More likely than not, there isn't a tiger behind us. So after eating these foods in large quantities we feel anxious, as if there is danger present. Anxiety and depression are closely linked because, as mentioned before, you can only stay anxious for so long and then you crash, falling into depression. It is a horrible cycle, only made worse by feeding your body with high-sugar foods.

Avoiding junk food is wonderful, but you have to eat something. Jack Challem tells us why it is so important to eat healthy, nutrient-dense foods.

> Nutrients provide the biological building blocks for brain chemicals called *neurotransmitters*, which affect how we think and feel. . . . When you don't eat enough high-quality *neuronutrients*—literally, "brain

nutrients"—your body cannot make adequate amounts of mood-enhancing neurotransmitters. . . . Your body needs vitamins, protein, and other nutrients to make the brain chemicals that help you think clearly, maintain a good mood, and act in socially acceptable ways.[9]

Julia Ross M.A., in her book, *The Mood Cure*, similarly speaks of nutritional impact on the neurotransmitter, serotonin. Tryptophan, which is found in eggs, poultry, beef, pork, and dairy products, is converted into serotonin. So to have enough of this mood regulator we must consume tryptophan in our diet. Many people do not get adequate amounts of tryptophan because animals today are not fed like our ancestor's animals were. Many animals today are fed on corn, which is low in tryptophan.[10] So America's trend of increased depression could be explained, at least partially, by our eating habits. Farm fresh, back-to-basic foods is what we desperately need.

I have always been a big promoter of exercise. Taking care of your body gives you a feeling of self-accomplishment and pride, which increases the positive thoughts you have about yourself. Anything you can do to increase your activity level will help. Health guidelines for Americans in 2005 include: Exercise thirty minutes per day for a minimum level. Exercise sixty minutes per day to maintain weight and prevent weight gain, and exercise sixty to ninety minutes per day to lose weight.[11] I am less concerned about the exact number of minutes per day. Rather, do what you can to increase you current activity level. Find what works for you. Some run, and some go to a gym. I prefer exercise videos. If you can do nothing but walk up and down your stairs a few times a day, then do it. Just get moving and you will feel better.

Exercise releases endorphins—which make us happy. They are the body's natural pain killer.[12] If you notice, the words endorphin and morphine look and sound similar. Endorphins mask pain because they are structurally similar to morphine.[13] I suppose our Maker instilled this mechanism in our body to ease discomfort because human beings have not always been blessed to have modern medicine. Exercise is not the only thing that increases your endorphin level. A variety of different foods, pain, falling in love, meditation, sunlight, and music will also cause this endorphin release.[14]

Exercise and nutrition work hand in hand when it comes to endorphins because both exercise and certain foods induce them; yet specific nutrients need to be ingested to actually create the chemical makeup of endorphins. Research shows that an intake of two amino acids, L-phenylalanine, and D-phenylalanine among a diet high in protein can help boost endorphin numbers.[15] "Endorphin building requires a big, consistent supply of high-protein foods like fish, eggs, cottage cheese, and chicken. . . . Lots of fresh vegetables and good fats are also vital. Vegetables are loaded with the vitamins and minerals that your brain needs to convert protein into the endorphins."[16]

Find a form of exercise you enjoy. Learn to love whole grains, fresh fruits, and vegetables. They give you long-lasting energy, help your mind think clearer, provide building blocks for neurotransmitters and endorphins, and on top of everything else you will be blessed because you have followed God's commandments.

Take Action:

- Eat Healthy. Do what you can to eliminate empty calories while increasing whole grains, legumes, and fruits and vegetables in your diet. Eat about the same time every day to stabilize your blood sugar and provide adequate energy. Quit using drugs, energy drinks, food, or other substances to self-medicate.

- Exercise. Exercise thirty minutes five times per week. Do the best you can to increase your activity level from what it is now.

- Consider taking supplements. Visit with your physician about taking a fish oil or Vitamin D supplement.

Professional Insights

Mike was in his midthirties. He had sought out counseling primarily from the urging of supportive friends and family. He was skeptical as to whether visiting with a counselor would lead to any benefit in his life. Mike started telling his story with, "I just can't seem to get things to work out." He seemed to have struggled in most areas of his life for many years. He had a broken and inconsistent work history. He couldn't seem to focus and stay on track with significant work projects. He vacillated with inconsistent sleep patterns, either being unable to sleep or wanting to simply stay in bed. He was divorced and had two young daughters, which he visited infrequently. A primary reason for his limited time with his daughters was that he didn't have a home or apartment to bring them to.

Mike struggled to maintain any stability in his own life and recognized his inability to provide a stable influence for his children, who lived with their mother, because Mike lived in the basement of his parent's home.

What very quickly jumped out to me about Mike's circumstance and symptoms was his lifestyle. Unless he had picked up some work or an odd job, he rarely left his room in the basement. From what he described, Mike had spent minimal time in sunlight and fresh air for several months. His diet consisted of food that primarily came from convenience stores. He really couldn't remember the last time he had shopped in a grocery store or had fresh fruit or vegetables in his diet with any consistency. Mike verbalized that he knew his unhealthy habits where damaging to his body, yet they were his only source of joy.

Throughout our discussions, Mike frequently described himself in negative terms. His expressions were reflections of the thoughts that lingered in his mind day after day. As we continued to meet and discuss his history and experiences, it became clear that he had struggled with depression for most of his adult life. It had never dawned on him that he struggled with an identifiable and very treatable illness. He had simply assumed he was "flawed" and that other people were just smarter, better, or luckier than he. Mike had learned to self-medicate with comfort foods and energy drinks because they momentarily eased the real emotional turmoil he struggled with.

I began teaching Mike to recognize the harmful and self-destructive patterns he had fallen into trying to simply cope with his emotional darkness. Though skeptical, he began to accept my challenge to try a different way. Mike's first task was to drastically change his lifestyle. I encouraged him to begin exercising and to start eating a healthy diet rich in fresh fruits and vegetables. I helped him to learn to recognize and rewrite the negative thought patterns he had come to dwell on. Over time, Mike began to recognize the benefits of change and the darkness of his depression began to fade.

HUGS

"But behold, the Lord hath redeemed my soul from hell; I have beheld his glory, and I am encircled about eternally in the arms of his love."

—2 Nephi 1:15

The influence of a hug is more powerful than you may know. A long, firm hug will make your body release endorphins. Their morphine-like quality helps to mask pain.[17] Strange as it may seem, when a small child skins his knee, a mother's hug really may help the child feel better physically.

Maria Meiners, known as the "Manifesting Muse" says,

> There is a power that each one of us holds in his or her own two arms. A tremendous power that is often completely overlooked or ignored. It has the ability to change someone's mood, influence decisions, change relationships and even affect the entire world at large. I'm talking about the power of a hug . . . On a purely physical level, our skin is our largest sensory organ, having hundreds of sensory receptors per square inch. A hug stimulates those receptors, increasing circulation and even lowering blood pressure. Hugging can also release endorphins—feel good hormones that improve mood. . . . Studies show that humans need a minimum of 8 hugs a day to stay healthy and 12 or more for growth. Considering that many people can't remember the last time they gave or received a hug, it's no wonder that so many people are trudging through life rather than really living.[18]

Kathleen Keating, author of *The Hug Therapy*, illustrates the many benefits of a hug: "Touch is not only nice. It's needed. Scientific research supports the theory that stimulation by touch is absolutely necessary for our physical as well as our emotional well-being. . . . Touch is used to help relieve pain and depression and anxiety, to bolster patients' will to live, to help premature babies—who have been deprived of touch in their incubators—grow and thrive."[19]

Growing up, if my siblings or I were acting gloomy, my mother would march up to us and say in a pouty voice, "Have you not had enough hugs today?" Then she would give us a big squeeze. It always worked. Hug your kids, your spouse, or anyone (with their permission). It will make both of you feel better. Hug long and hug often. And remember you are always eternally encircled in the Savior's loving arms (2 Nephi 1:15).

There is no person on the face of this earth who doesn't have someone to embrace them. Our Savior's hands are always reached out toward us. Tad R. Callister of the Seventy in his book, *The Infinite Atonement*, states:

> Elder Orson F. Whitney experienced such a glorious moment when he saw a marvelous manifestation of the Savior. In his dream, he

said, "I ran [to meet Him] . . . , fell at his feet, clasped Him around the knees, and begged Him to take me with him. I shall never forget the kind and gentle manner in which He stopped, raised me up, *and embraced me.* It was so vivid, so real. I felt the very warmth of his body, and He held me in his arms." Who would not long for that warmth, that embrace? . . . Even in God's moments of anger, his arms are stretched out still, anxiously enticing the repentant soul.

Callister goes on to say, "Elder Neal A. Maxwell suggests that the prime reason the Savior personally acts as the gatekeeper of the celestial kingdom is not to exclude people, but to personally welcome and embrace those who have made it back home. It is a touching, intimate thought."[20]

The Atonement of Christ is not only for sins committed. The healing power of the Atonement can heal addiction, heartache, pain, regret, and depression. The embrace of His atoning power has the ability to heal your troubled heart.

Take Action:

- Don't be afraid to ask for a hug. Don't be afraid to give hugs either.

- Enlist support. Have your support person check on you daily. It may be helpful to have them ask you how you are feeling that day based on a scale of 1–10 by asking, "What are your numbers today?" (suicidal=10, happy=0) That way when you say a high number, you know a hug and help is on the way.

Professional Insights

Stephanie appeared to be an average sixteen-year-old. She had numerous friends and was involved in many extracurricular activities. Outwardly, she appeared to be a confident intelligent young women, but on the inside, she was suffering immensely. Most mornings she lacked the desire or energy to even get out of bed. The only reason she did the things she did was out of fear of failure or rejection.

Although a pretty girl, Stephanie lacked a healthy self-esteem. As a child, she had been physically and verbally abused by her father. Because of his temper, she was in constant fear of doing something wrong. He always told her how ugly and stupid she was. If she made any mistake, she was belittled and occasionally hit. Even though her mother eventually remarried a good man, Stephanie carried the burden of those damaging events with her as she grew.

Stephanie was a perfectionist by nature. As she matured, she became more and more critical of herself. She often felt that if she didn't do well at everything, she would let her family down. She only felt good about herself when she got perfect grades, made the basketball team, or when someone complimented her.

When I first met with Stephanie, it was clear she was suffering with depression. She had been suffering with it for many years. We began working through her past abuse and correcting the negative thoughts that came from unrealistic expectations. I asked her what she had done in the past to help relieve her symptoms. Stephanie explained that she had a wonderful relationship with her mother. She said that sometimes her depression was so severe it made her physically sick. It was during these times that her mother simply held her. Sometimes her mother would sit next to her in her bed and just hold her or stroke her hair. The embrace of her mother always helped her feel better and gave her the peace and comfort she needed to face another day. Although Stephanie had issues to work through, I found it interesting that something as simple as a hug was an essential part of her recovery.

EARLY TO BED, EARLY TO RISE

Doctrine and Covenants 88:124 says, "Cease to be idle; cease to be unclean; cease to find fault one with another; cease to sleep longer than is needful; retire to thy bed early, that ye may not be weary; arise early, that your bodies and your minds may be invigorated." "Early to bed, early to rise" is more than just a catchy phrase. Laurie Winn Carson, author of *The Sunlight Solution*, explicated the connection between awakening time and depression. "Sleeping late in the morning allows for too much REM (rapid eye movement) sleep, which has been linked to an increased risk of developing depression. Studies have shown that depression can be linked to the time of waking, with a lower incidence of depression among those who get up before sunrise."[21] Interestingly enough, in scripture it is mentioned thirty-five times that prophets did great things early in the morning. I love it when science discovers truths that have already been given to us by revelation.

Getting adequate sleep may be just as important. I would wager that the cause of many of the cases of postpartum depression is partially due to the lack of sleep women get from being up in the night with their newborns. In his book, *The Depression Cure*, Dr. Ilardi discusses the correlation between sleep deprivation and depression.

> Recent advances in the neurosciences have brought the discovery that adequate sleep is indispensable for both physical and mental well-being. . . . In fact, it is only during sleep that the body and brain have a chance to do their major repair work—to undo the subtle damage suffered by millions of cells over the course of each day—and to perform a daily tune-up so things continue running smoothly. Sleep is what keeps us firing on all cylinders.
>
> Because sleep is so essential to our well-being, it takes only a few nights of deprivation before adverse effects start piling up: memory and concentration wane; mood turns irritable; judgment grows poor; reaction times slow; coordination deteriorates; energy dims; and immune function declines. . . .
>
> Sadly, sleep disturbance and depression go hand in hand. Not only is disordered sleep one of the telltale symptoms of depression, but it also plays a major role in triggering the illness . . . Not surprisingly, before the onset of depression, four out of five people suffer from some form of sleep disturbance.
>
> The implications are clear: Anything we can do to improve our sleep can help combat depression and render the disorder less likely to occur in the future.[22]

In nearly every phase of life there is an excuse for pushing sleep aside. Teenagers want to be up late at night with their friends. College-age individuals stay up late studying or socializing. Young couples are up in the night with their babies. From this point on, people are either waiting up for their teenagers to get home by curfew or busy with work. By the time you reach retirement age, the house is so quiet you can't sleep!

Some people with depression insist they sleep too much or feel tired all the time. Dr. Ilardi explains, "As it turns out, many cases of depressive hypersomnia result from inefficient sleep: multiple awakenings through the night and a reduced amount of restorative slow-wave sleep. Because people with this problem get such poor quality sleep, they may find themselves in bed for twelve or fourteen hours a night, and yet still feeling tired."[23]

Even our Father in Heaven emphasized the importance of rest when He designated the Sabbath day, a day of rest. While there sometimes isn't anything we can do about a situation that challenges sleep, at least recognizing the importance of sleep can help you make any possible changes to improve it.

Take Action:

- Get adequate sleep. Strive to get eight hours of sleep each night. Dim the lights an hour before you plan to sleep. Try to have a set bedtime and wake time because our bodies thrive on consistency. Avoid exercising in the evening. Write out your negative or anxious thoughts and replace them before bed. This way your mind will not keep you awake.

FIND BALANCE IN LIFE—"GET BUSY," OR "COOL IT, RELAX"

In her program, *You Deserve to be Happy*, Ellen Kreidman discusses the power of action. She tells us to simply do what a happy person would do, even if we don't feel up to it. She explains how often it is the act of "doing" that makes us happy. It seems backward, but—believe me—it works. Think about the example of exercise. If you waited until you felt in the mood to exercise, you may not do it as often. But if you get up out of bed, pull on your sneakers and get outside for that morning jog, eventually you do feel good and you are glad you worked out.[24]

I put this to the test my first year in college. I was working as a certified nurse assistant at a care center. It was my first real job (aside from the jobs I did with my family). Sometimes I dreaded getting up for work at five in the morning. I had all sorts of negative thoughts that I had to change each day. I decided that even though I didn't feel like going to work, I would act like I was happy to go to work. I had to ask myself, *What would a happy person do?* I had a spunky bubbly friend in high school so I tried to imitate her persona. Once I got to work, I got a big smile on my face and greeted all of my coworkers with, "Good morning, isn't it a great day?" (I'm sure they all thought I was crazy saying such things so early in the morning.) I tried being helpful and smiley all day. I joked with the residents and other workers. I whistled while I walked up and down the halls to answer call lights. Before long, I actually was enjoying myself at work. I had to do this every morning, but the results were amazing. I started out every morning feeling tired and grumpy, but by the end of my "pretend" happy day, I was actually, truly happy! Plus, my happiness was contagious and the other workers seemed to catch the bug and the day was more pleasant for everyone. Don't wait for the feelings to come before you do the action. It is usually the action that creates the feelings.

Use up that adrenaline that your thoughts may have triggered. Just getting up off the couch and cleaning your house puts that energy to use. Exercise falls into this category as well. To put a spiritual spin on things, the scripture in John 3:21 says, "But he that doeth truth cometh to the light, that his deeds may be made manifest, that they are wrought in God." Doing truth brings light. It brings happiness. Living the commandments of God will bring happiness faster than anything else I can think of. Maybe that is why everyone says that service brings joy. Getting out and helping someone else is a sure-fire way to push away those self-absorbed, negative thoughts because you're busy thinking of someone else.

You might be thinking, *Get busy? I don't think I can get any busier!* Some people need motivation to get off the couch, but there are also those whose lives will be blessed if they simply slow down. You will have to determine which category you fall under.

President Dieter F. Uchtdorf related this message in the 2010 October general conference.

> Let's be honest; it's rather easy to be busy. We all can think up a list of tasks that will overwhelm our schedules. Some might even think that their self-worth depends on the length of their to-do list. They flood the open spaces in their time with lists of meetings and minutia—even during times of stress and fatigue. Because they unnecessarily complicate their lives, they often feel increased frustration, *diminished joy*, and too little sense of meaning in their lives. It is said that any virtue when taken to an extreme can become a vice. Over scheduling our days would certainly qualify for this. There comes a point where milestones can become millstones and ambitions, albatrosses around our necks.[25]

My family was blessed with an angel on earth. My youngest brother has Down Syndrome. A common phrase that escapes his lips is, "Cool it, relax." If anyone is hurrying him along or getting after him for something he did wrong, he will bluntly tell them, "Cool it, relax." This usually brings a smile to our faces and reminds us that nothing is worth getting too upset over.

So to those of you out there who are perfectionists, overachievers, or super busybodies, I say . . . . "Cool it, relax!" Weed your tight schedule of unnecessary activities. Let the basic principles of the gospel help you prioritize what is most important and what you can do without. President Uchtdorf concludes his address by saying, "Let us simplify our lives a little. Let us make the changes necessary to refocus our lives on the sublime beauty of the simple, humble path of Christian discipleship—the path that leads always toward a life of meaning, gladness, and peace."[26] From past experience, I have noticed that my depression was the worst during times when I had nothing to do, and also during the times I had too much to do. Balance is the key.

Take Action:

- Act like a happy person would act. Get out of your cave. Go for a walk. Spend time with friends and family. A common response to depression is to simply hide. Isolating oneself from supportive friends and family usually feeds the problem and contributes to the downward spiral of depression. You might not feel like doing these things but doing them anyway will improve your condition. Fake it till you make it.

- Find Balance. If you are too busy, balance your life by eliminating unessential activities. You can do this by writing down your regular daily or weekly activities and number them according to your priorities. If you have difficulty getting motivated:

1. **Start simple.** Make yourself do one activity a day and work up to more as you feel comfortable. Ask a friend to do things with you. For example, you are more likely to exercise if you know a friend is meeting you at the gym.
2. **Get going in the morning.** Even if you don't have a job or an appointment to get to, start the day off right. Get up; eat a healthy breakfast; clean up. Look your best no matter what you are doing with your day. If you feel good about you, you will feel good in general.

Professional Insights

Brian was an ambitious man. He was always busy trying to balance the demands of his full-time job, a farm, his family, and random businesses he was involved in. He never missed his children's ball games or musical competitions, even when long distance travel was required. There was never a free moment in his schedule. Any spare afternoon that presented itself was quickly filled with exciting adventures up the mountain or hobbies with his children. Often the hours in the day did not match up with the hours of activities he was involved in. When something had to give, it was usually his sleep. During the farming seasons, he worked all day at his job and then bailed the hay all night. It was not unusual for him to wake up at four in the morning to travel to one of his kid's tournaments or to take the Scouts fishing. Not only did he overbook his schedule, but being a shift-worker, his sleep was inconsistent. One week he would work days, another week he would work nights. Year after year he pushed on, thinking that sleep was not as important as all the other things he was required to do.

Although Brian was a cheerful person and had an overall positive demeanor, his physical and mental health began to suffer from his lack of sleep. It became most noticeable when a sudden illness took him by surprise. Still, he didn't want to take off work so he pushed through the pain. As he feared that his illness might be permanent, a horrible knot of depression began to grow. The thought of living in that condition his entire life nearly consumed him. His anxiety over the situation began to increase.

At the onset of his illness, Brian was beginning his week of night shifts. He would come home from work in the morning and try to sleep but his pain and anxiety made it difficult. For nearly five days he worked all night and slept only a couple hours in between shifts. At the end of the week he was completely worn down. Although he had never experienced anxiety or depression before this incident, he found himself in a dark and anxious state. He could not even think clearly to make a decision about what to do next.

His loving wife recognized that his sleep-deprivation was worsening his condition exponentially. Although no medication or treatment existed for his illness, they met with their family physician who prescribed a benzodiazepine (anti-anxiety medication) to relax him enough that he could sleep. A few days after taking the medication, he was a new man. With several full nights of sleep he could think clearly. He recognized a need to bring order and balance into his life along with getting adequate sleep. With his depression and anxiety under wrap, he and his wife began searching for possible ways to reduce the symptoms of his illness. And once he embraced a healthy sleeping pattern, he rarely needed the anti-anxiety medication.

MUSIC

Another piece of advice from my mother was to listen to uplifting music. Hymns have a way of getting into your heart and invigorating you. Elder Boyd K. Packer of the Quorum of the Twelve taught that each of us should memorize a hymn. This aids in controlling any inappropriate or negative thought. Once a bad thought comes into our mind, singing that memorized hymn will push the negative thought away. He says,

> A wise man once said, "Music is one of the most forceful instruments for governing the mind." Whether it governs in a positive way or a negative way is determined by what it brings onto the stage of your mind. If you can say that a song is spiritually inspiring or that it urges you to see yourself in a more noble perspective, the music is worthwhile. If it merely entertains or lifts your spirits, then it also has a useful place.[27]

Hymns are not the only high-quality music available to lift your spirits. I have found songs that make me feel energized. I love the music from the Broadway musical *Wicked*. The way the orchestra blends together and with song titles such as "Defying Gravity,"[28] it's no wonder I feel limitless. I can be having a rotten day and once I turn it on and crank up the volume, I can clean my house faster. I feel happy and energetic. I forget my worries and concentrate on the beautiful music. Aside from that, peaceful music also has a way of calming those internal chemical exchanges that build up inside due to our negative and anxious thoughts.

I grew up on a farm and from an early age I participated in planting and harvesting the crops. My favorite task was cutting hay in the swather. It had a nice cab with air conditioning and I would turn up the radio and sing my lungs out all day long. Being outdoors, helping my dad, and having meditation time all made the farming experience a joy; however, I feel that those melodies I would sing along with really made the blues disappear.

In Doctrine and Covenants 25:12 it says, "For my soul *delighteth* in the song of the heart; yea, the song of the righteous is a prayer unto me, and it shall be answered with a blessing upon their head." *Delight* is a fun word because the word "light" is built right in. Try listening to good music while doing housework, gardening, or any other daily task. Just see how much faster you get it done and how much more you enjoy doing it. It is a simple test to prove how powerful music can be. Even crying babies are often calmed when you begin to sing to them. It works.

Take Action:

- Use music to improve your mood. Memorize a hymn. Listen to uplifting music when you feel your mood declining. Pay attention to how you feel with various genres of music. Gravitate toward music that inspires, calms, and uplifts. If you have a musical talent, continue to develop and use it.

MENTAL TIME TRAVEL

"I had no shoes and complained, until I met a man with no feet."
—Indian Proverb

Perspective has everything to do with happiness and how easily positive thoughts come to you. That is why mental time travel, or imagining yourself in a more difficult time or situation, automatically helps you to feel more content with your current situation.

For example, my grandmother once lived next to a sweet ninety-two-year-old lady. This neighbor, who was normally fairly independent, had recently lost her ability to climb stairs or even read because of her fading vision and aging body. One day while the two of them were visiting on the porch, my grandma recalls her neighbor saying, "What I wouldn't give to be eighty again." Hearing that comment made my grandma more grateful than she had ever been to be sixty years old—twenty years younger than her neighbor's wish. She became more satisfied with her own age based on this new perspective.

So if you look in the mirror and begin to get depressed because you see a few wrinkles and gray hairs, just move forward in time and imagine being ninety years old. That mental image helps you replace negative thoughts about yourself by thinking how healthy and vibrant your body is now compared to what it could be.

Someone whose husband is gone a lot for work might feel discouraged or alone. All you have to do is imagine how lonely you would feel if your spouse died. This imagery makes you instantly content with what little time you do get with them. An elderly widow may feel less discouraged by the loss of her husband when she thinks about individuals who lost a spouse early in marriage. If you have lost a loved one at any time, you can always imagine a worse situation, such as never knowing that person and missing the memories you made with them.

After many long nights of being up with sick children, I have found myself getting irritable. When this happens, all I have to do is imagine going through the same situation, only several hundred years ago. Somehow our ancestors raised a handful of children in a one-room, dirt-floored log cabin, without the convenience of modern medicine. Instantly that simple remembrance allows me to regain a positive attitude.

Achy joints suddenly become a blessing when you imagine yourself bedridden. The clutter in your house no longer bothers you when you imagine being left homeless from a natural disaster. For those who are paralyzed, wheelchairs become luxuries allowing mobility instead of restraints when they imagine living in another country without these modern devices. You can always have a more positive outlook, no matter what circumstance you are in, by simply changing your perspective.

Possibly the last thing you want to hear is that someone has it worse than you. You might feel like you *are* the worst situation. I do not wish to minimize your sorrow. Your trials are real and absolutely heart-wrenching. It is a big deal what you're going through. Experience your trial and allow yourself to feel that pain. When enough time has passed and you are tired of feeling sad and angry, you can then begin changing your perspective.

Take Action:

- Count your blessings. Choose a couple of situations in your life that discourage you. Mentally spend time in a worse situation until your perspective is changed and you feel greater content with your current situation. Doctrine and Covenants 122:8 says "The Son of Man hath descended below them all. Art though greater than he?"

NOTES

1. *Teachings of Presidents of the Church: George Albert Smith* (Salt Lake City, UT: Intellectual Reserve, 2011), xiv.

2. Jennifer Nuckols, "Truths and Lies," *Ensign*, Oct. 2009, 62–65, emphasis added.

3. Burns, *Feeling Good*, 12–13.

4. Ibid., 48.

5. Ibid., 42–43, 216.

6. Bruce K. Fordham, "Think About What You Are Thinking About," *Ensign*, Apr. 2009, 68–69.

7. Jill Ammon-Wexler, PhD, "The Unbelievable Power of YOUR Brain," (Ravino, 2007), accessed February 27, 2012 from http://www.buildmind-power.com/library/brainpower/article8.htm.

8. Ellen Kreidman, PhD, *Light His Fire: How to Keep Your Man Passionately and Hopelessly in Love With You* (New York, NY: Dell Publishing, 1989), 16–17.

9. Challem and Werbach, *The Food-Mood Solution*, 4–5.

10. Julia Ross, MA, *The Mood Cure: The 4-Step Program to Take Charge of Your Emotions—Today* (New York, NY: The Penguin Group, 2002), 27.

11. Ruth F. Craven and Constance J. Hirnle, *Fundamentals of Nursing: Human Health and Function: 5th Edition* (Philadelphia, Pennsylvania: Lippincott Williams & Wilkins, 2007), 973 Box 39–1.

12. Lewis, *Medical-Surgical Nursing*, 118.

13. Jeff Goldberg, *Anatomy of a Scientific Discovery* (New York, NY: Bantam Books, 1988), 5.

14. Ross, *The Mood Cure*, 100–101, 113.

15. Ibid., 106.

16. Ibid., 112.

17. Goldberg, *Anatomy of a Scientific Discovery*, 5.

18. Maria Meiners, "Law of Attraction Lesson—The Power You Hold in Your Own Two Arms," accessed Dec. 7, 2009, from http://ezinearticles.com/?Law-of-Attraction-Lesson-The-Power-You-Hold-in-Your-Own-Two-Arms&id=2504390.

19. Kathleen Keating, *The Hug Therapy Book* (Minneapolis, MN: CompCare Publications, 1983), 1.

20. Tad R. Callister, *The Infinite Atonement* (Salt Lake City, UT: Deseret Book, 2000), 27–28.

21. Laurie W. Carlson, *The Sunlight Solution: Why More Sun Exposure and Vitamin D Are Essential to Your Health* (Amherst, NY: Prometheus Books, 2009), 165.

22. Stephen S. Ilardi, PhD, *The Depression Cure—The 6-Step Program to Beat Depression Without Drugs* (Cambridge, MA: Da Capo Press, 2009), 193–194.

23. Ibid., 210–211.

24. Ellen Kreidman, PhD (speaker), *You Deserve To Be Happy* (Cassette Recording), (Commerce, CA: Mega Systems International, 1996), Tape 1 and 6.

25. Dieter F. Uchtdorf, "Of Things That Matter Most," *Ensign*, Nov. 2010, 19–22, emphasis added.

26. Ibid.

27. Boyd K. Packer, "Worthy Music, Worthy Thoughts," *New Era*, Apr. 2008, 8–11.

28. Stephen Schwartz, and Winnie Holzman, *Wicked The Musical* Soundtrack CD, recorded, November 3, 2003 (New York, NY: Right Track Studios), 11.

Chapter Four

VOICES

"But ye are a chosen generation, a royal priesthood, an holy nation, a peculiar people; that ye should shew forth the praises of him who hath called you out of darkness into his marvelous light."
—1 Peter 2:9

I cannot recall for certain, but I believe it was my mother who first introduced the idea of separate voices to me. You know—all the different voices inside your head? I'm not suggesting you are crazy, it's just that not all the voices you hear are your own. For example, one voice you hear is your own physical voice. The one that comes out of your mouth. Another voice is what I like to call your "head voice." This is the one that you think with. It is usually a pretty mean one too. It is that voice that says, *You ought to drop a few pounds,* when you're looking at yourself in the mirror. The voice which says, *What if my husband gets in a wreck on the way home from work?* Or, *Everyone else seems to get this algebra stuff. I am so stupid!* No one else hears this dialogue you have with yourself but it greatly dictates your thoughts, thus controlling your mood.

Another voice is the echoing words from family or friends that randomly come into mind. I know there are some of you out there who can still clearly hear in your mother's exact tone and style, the phrase, "Remember who you are!" Sometimes this old warning conveniently comes when you're about to do something foolish. Another example: Every time I am at someone's house for dinner and I don't like what they are serving, I distinctly hear my mother's voice say, "It doesn't matter if you don't like it. You need to be polite and eat what you are served when you are a guest at someone's house." If these old voices weren't bad enough, we all have the actual voices of family and friends, hurling expectations and "shoulds" our way. Maybe you still live at home and your parents are still telling you what they think you should do. Or maybe you have a roommate, a spouse, or even children telling you things you should do or change. You may have a neighbor say to you, "Well, when I was Relief Society president, I did it this way . . . " The outside voices go on and on. Not all criticism is bad and I don't mean to harp on parents' instruction. It's just that life can get confusing wondering which voice to listen to.

There is yet another voice—the voice of Satan—always creeping in your head giving you bad thoughts, telling you that you're worthless and other lies. His voice is often disguised and small. He slithers in unannounced. Sometimes he works through your "head voice," feeding you lies and tempting you to say negative things about yourself or others. Luckily we have a contrasting voice—the Holy Ghost. A voice that is still and small, which guides, testifies, comforts, and enlightens.

So between your physical voice, your head voice, your family and friends' voices, Satan's voice, and the voice of the Holy Ghost, one can quickly see how complicated it is to control your thoughts while tuning out the insignificant voices so the Holy Ghost can be heard. Controlling your thoughts is an ongoing process of enhancing your ability to push out negative thoughts while increasing your sensitivity to the Spirit.

I'd like to make a suggestion that with the help of the Holy Ghost, you become the orange-vested traffic controller of your voices. Just as you learned the importance of having realistic expectations, you must also only allow good voices in your mind. Don't let your head voice tell you that you're fat or whatever it may be. That's rude! You wouldn't say that to anyone else. Why say it to yourself? Don't let your neighbor's vocal suggestions become what you must live by. And most of all, don't tolerate the voice of Satan entering in your mind. With all of them out of the way, the Holy Ghost will have free passage.

Have you ever wondered whether an idea or thought was yours or the Holy Ghost's? Sometimes it doesn't matter. Whatever thoughts are good, virtuous, and wholesome—or is an idea that leads to something good, virtuous, and wholesome—are thoughts or ideas that ought to be entertained.

I have had times in my life where my depression seemed related to a decision I was trying to make. I had a difficult time deciding whether it was the Holy Ghost telling me the decision I chose was wrong or if it was Satan just doing what he does best—making me feel discouraged. Beginning my junior year in high school, I struggled with a career choice. I had decided on nursing but I never felt very sure about it. I began college with nursing in mind. When it came time to apply to the program, my depression was nearly the worst it had ever been. I had prayed over and over whether it was the right choice or not. I never really got a strong "Yes" but I didn't get a "No" either. The following scripture helped me separate regular fears and anxieties from life stressors versus promptings from the Holy Spirit.

Doctrine and Covenants 8:2 says, "Yea, behold, I will tell you in your mind and in your heart, by the Holy Ghost, which shall come upon you and which shall dwell in your heart." Satan can put thoughts into your head, but he cannot put feelings into your heart. After much prayer and fasting, I realized the feeling in my heart was to press forward. I still wasn't sure that I would enjoy nursing or that it was going to be the best career choice to fit my life, but I knew my heart said to press forward in that direction. The feelings of sorrow, despair, anxiety, darkness, worthlessness, anguish, and hopelessness are the result of a depressed mood. They are *not* feelings that the Holy Ghost uses to tell you an idea or choice is wrong. The Holy Ghost may use an uneasiness feeling or a sense of "this is not right," or "I shouldn't be here," but he never makes you feel worthless, hopeless, or dark. He warns; He doesn't terrorize. If you have sinned, he will leave a feeling of guilt in attempt to motivate you to change. Guilt is not the same as worthlessness. The empty, hopeless feelings that come with guilt are from Satan. He would love nothing more than to discourage you to the point that you feel unworthy of the Atonement.

If you are having a difficult time determining the voices you hear, just ask yourself, "How did that make me feel?" If the answer is belittled, worthless, hopeless, or depressed, stop those voices at once. If they are feelings of guilt, promptings to change, heartfelt sorrow for sin, and so on, recognize them as the powerful influence of the Holy Ghost. Please be careful as you listen and discern. Sometimes Satan mimics the Lord's pattern of teaching in his efforts to influence us.

While my husband attended medical school in Missouri, we had the privilege of belonging to Bishop Doman's ward. Not only was he our bishop, but also our institute teacher as well. I learned many things from this respectable man during our years there. Bishop Doman taught me this truth in institute one day. He said, "A close look at the Adversary's strategies reveals that he uses the same methods as the Lord to get our attention, only he moves us in the exact opposite direction, away from the Lord and toward captivity. He is the polar opposite."[1] Examine the following approaches used both by Satan and our Heavenly Father as illustrated by the following scriptures.

Method	Satan	The Lord
Whispers	2 Nephi 28:22 "And behold, others he flattereth away, and telleth them there is no hell; and he saith unto them: I am no devil, for there is none— and thus he whispereth in their ears, until he grasps them with his awful chains, from whence there is no deliverance."	Words of Mormon 1:7 "And I do this for a wise purpose, for thus it whispereth me, according to the workings of the Spirit of the Lord which is in me. And now, I do not know all things; but the Lord knoweth all things which are to come; wherefore, he worketh in me to do according to his will."
Entices	Moroni 7:12 "Wherefore, all things which are good cometh of God; and that which is evil cometh of the devil; for the devil is an enemy unto God, and fighteth against him continually, and inviteth and enticeth to sin, and to do that which is evil continually."	Moroni 7:13 "But behold, that which is of God inviteth and enticeth to do good continually; wherefore, everything which inviteth and enticeth to do good, and to love God, and to serve him, is inspired of God."
Teaches	2 Nephi 32:8 continued " . . . for the evil spirit teacheth not a man to pray, but teacheth him that he must not pray."	2 Nephi 32:8 "For if ye would hearken unto the Spirit which teacheth a man to pray ye would know that ye must pray;"

Gently Leads	2 Nephi 28:21 "And others will he pacify, and lull them away into carnal security, that they will say: All is well in Zion; yea, Zion prospereth, all is well—and thus the devil cheateth their souls, and leadeth them away carefully down to hell."	Jacob 4:15 "And now I, Jacob, am led on by the Spirit unto prophesying; for I perceive by the workings of the Spirit which is in me, that by the stumbling of the Jews they will reject the stone upon which they might build and have safe foundation."
Seals	Alma 34:35 "For behold, if ye have procrastinated the day of your repentance even until death, behold, ye have become subjected to the spirit of the devil, and he doth seal you his; therefore, the Spirit of the Lord hath withdrawn from you, and hath no place in you, and the devil hath all power over you; and this is the final state of the wicked."	Mosiah 5:15 "Therefore, I would that ye should be steadfast and immovable, always abounding in good works, that Christ, the Lord God Omnipotent, may seal you his, that you may be brought to heaven, that ye may have everlasting salvation and eternal life, through the wisdom, and power, and justice, and mercy of him who created all things, in heaven and in earth, who is God above all. Amen."

My bishop explained these scriptures using a linear visual.

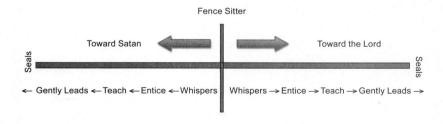

Bishop Doman emphasized that we must choose; we can't be neutral or in the middle ground where it is not as clear to discern. Notice that if you are a "fence sitter," you are in an extremely dangerous area because you are trying to discern between two whispers. Alma 30:8

says, "For thus saith the scripture: choose ye this day, whom ye will serve." Bishop Doman concludes his remarks with, "Let's choose once and for all, to be where it is clear, where it is evident which voice is which. The voice of the Spirit helps illuminate where the line is; it clarifies things, and invites us to reach toward God while fleeing further away from temptation and evil. The voice of the devil blurs where the line is. He distorts truth and blinds us. *Listen to the Spirit.*"[2]

We must flee from darkness and from Satan's grasp by continually seeking for the Lord's light. Again, having the constant companionship of the Holy Ghost will help us understand the voices we encounter. He will help us learn what kind of things we should think about ourselves. As we strive to live the commandments with all the energy we possess we will invite the spirit to dwell with us. Then in this seemingly confusing realm of voices and temptations, we will see clearly and we will find the light we desire.

Take Action:

- Learn to recognize how the Spirit speaks to you. **Learning to recognize and listen to the promptings of the Spirit is an ability that grows with practice and experience.**

- Ask for a Priesthood blessing.

- Pray and work for the gift of discernment.

NOTES

1. Danion Doman, Personal Communication, Kirksville, Missouri, September 28, 2010.

2. Ibid.

Chapter Five

TRIAL OR TRANSGRESSION?

S ome depression may come from problems we have caused by our own actions, while other pain may come from events completely out of our control. We can learn to eliminate behavior that brings upon us sadness while accepting and learning from trials that God allows to happen to us—those trials that bring with them pain but ultimately growth and understanding if handled with the right attitude.

WICKEDNESS NEVER WAS HAPPINESS

"There is no tragedy in death, only in sin."[1]

—Spencer W. Kimball

"Wickedness never was happiness" (Alma 41:10), a phrase taught by the Prophet Alma to the inhabitants of ancient America, is as applicable today as it was then. This simple truth does not say that if you are unhappy then you are wicked (something I used to believe). It simply means that you will not find the happiness you desire by indulging in sin. That is why each person who is searching for peace and joy must first analyze his or her life. Ask yourself, "Are my actions in accordance with God's commandments? Am I keeping my covenants? Am I doing the best I can to live righteously?" Repenting of your sins must take place before true happiness can be found.

The weight of sin can be extremely unbearable. The added guilt from transgression feeds the fire of depression. A common lie Satan whispers is, "You are too far gone. You can't repent. It is too late for you." While repentance is painful and difficult, it is within your reach. Elder Jeffrey R. Holland states:

> I don't know what things may be troubling you personally, but even knowing how terrific you are and how faithfully you are living, I would be surprised if someone somewhere weren't troubled by a transgression or the temptation of transgression. To you, wherever you may be, I say, Come unto him and lay down your burden. Let him lift the load. Let him give peace to your soul. Nothing in this world is more burdensome than sin—it is the heaviest cross men and women ever bear.
>
> The world around us is an increasingly hostile and sinful place. Occasionally that splashes onto us, and perhaps, in the case of a few of you, it may be nearly drowning you. To anyone struggling under the burden of sin, I say again with the Prophet Joseph that God has "a forgiving disposition" (Lectures on Faith, 42). You can change. You can be helped. You can be made whole—whatever the problem. *All he asks is that you walk away from the darkness and come into the light,* his light, with meekness and lowliness of heart. That is at the heart of the gospel. That is the very center of our message. That is the beauty of redemption. Christ has "borne our griefs, and carried our sorrows," Isaiah declared, "and with his stripes we are healed;—if we want to be" (Isaiah 53:4–5; see also Mosiah 14:4–5).[2]

In the Book of Mormon we see how Alma the Younger uses the descriptive words of light and dark to explain his life with sin. "My soul hath been redeemed from the gall of bitterness and bonds of iniquity. *I was in the darkest abyss; but now I behold the marvelous light of God.* My soul was racked with eternal torment; but I am snatched, and my soul is pained no more" (Mosiah 27:29, emphasis added). Truly, wickedness never was happiness.

Take Action:

- Repent of sins committed. Seek counsel from your bishop if the sin is of a serious nature. Bring your life in harmony with your values and beliefs. One cannot do wrong and feel right.

- Forgive yourself. Once you have truly repented, forgive yourself and let go of the guilt.

Professional Insights

Early in my career as a therapist, I met a man who struggled with shifting and unstable changes in his mood. He was also deeply troubled with his own sense of spirituality. He met with me because he had come to recognize the depression in his life. It had plagued him for many years. The challenges he faced in managing his depression had taken a measurable toll on his interpersonal life as well. His marriage had suffered, and he felt inadequate as a parent. Like many who suffer from depression, he struggled with often unhealthy strategies to simply cope with the daily overwhelming shifts of emotion he experienced. He recognized many of his coping strategies as "sins," yet he felt the immediate relief he received from them outweighed the long-term negative consequences of his transgressions.

What was also a critical element in this good man's story, was how he had lost sight of the light he once enjoyed. This man had grown up in the light of the gospel. He had served as a missionary and enjoyed a temple marriage to his companion. He had served faithfully in many capacities in the Church. Unfortunately, in recent years, he had come to question his value and worth as a child of God. Like most of us, he struggled with the guilt he felt from his sins. In one discussion he expressed his belief, quite sincerely, that the gifts of the Savior's Atonement were extended to all—except himself. I struggled to distinguish whether his spiritual struggles were the result of his battle with depression, or whether his depression was the result of his loss of spiritual light.

Admittedly, our visits were often emotionally challenging for me personally as a therapist. His tendency to demean himself had become so habitual he barely recognized how pervasive it was in his thoughts and in his daily speech. The treatment goals we focused on were not only about overcoming the negative speech and changing some of the more basic elements of thought and lifestyle, but also on healing spiritually as well. In so many ways, he *knew* what to do but needed prompting and encouragement to return to the source of light he had previously enjoyed.

OPPOSITION IN ALL THINGS

A truth we have learned from the written word is that there is opposition in all things (2 Nephi 2:11). This was necessary for agency to exist, and we all know how important agency is. Technically we could never experience peace, joy, and happiness without knowing sorrow and grief. So as much as I'd love disappointment and pain to leave my life forever, it cannot be. Nor would the plan of our Father in Heaven even exist if it were this way.

Picture with me a stormy day. There is a chill in the wind. The sky is dark gray, covered in thick rain clouds. The sun is lost, hidden behind the murky billows. There is a musty, damp smell in the air. This gloomy picture painted by my imagination is how our lives may seem at times. We may ask ourselves, "Is there any good that comes from a dreary rainstorm?" Being raised in a family of farmers I can testify how important it is to receive precipitation. Storm clouds, as gloomy as they appear, provide much-needed rain for our crops. Nothing would ever grow if the rain clouds disappeared because rain would no longer fall upon the ground. So it is in our lives. How are we to grow? How are our testimonies supposed to be strengthened if we don't experience a few rain clouds? How do we become more like God if we do not learn to overcome our trials? How can our faith be strengthened if the sun is always in perfect view? Some of my most fervent prayers have been uttered when my depression was full force. When I thought I could not take it one more day. When I saw zero hope before me, and I felt utterly alone. This was the point where I would fall to my knees, cry my eyes out to an ever-patient and loving Father in Heaven, and plead with Him for help. It was also at those times that my testimony grew leaps and bounds as I learned to rely on the Lord through my trials. It humbled me and refined me.

Elder Joseph B. Wirthlin elaborates on the purpose of our suffering.

Learning to endure times of disappointment, suffering, and sorrow is part of our on-the-job training. These experiences, while often difficult to bear at the time, are precisely the kinds of experiences that stretch our understanding, build our character, and increase our compassion for others.

Because Jesus Christ suffered greatly, He understands our suffering. He understands our grief. We experience hard things so that we too may have increased compassion and understanding for others.

Remember the sublime words of the Savior to the Prophet Joseph Smith when he suffered with his companions in the smothering darkness of Liberty jail:

"My son, peace be unto they soul; thine adversity and thine

afflictions shall be but a small moment; and then if thou endure it well, God shall exalt thee on high; though shalt triumph over all they foes" (Doctrine and Covenants 121:7–8).

With that eternal perspective, Joseph took comfort from these words, and so can we. Sometimes the very moments that seem to overcome us with suffering are those that will ultimately suffer us to overcome.[3]

It is better to light a candle than curse the darkness.[4] Don't be angry because of your depression. Instead, search for ways to create light. My negative-prone personality, although bothersome to me, has been a blessing to others at times. I am more sensitive and understanding of other people; whereas, I may not be as sympathetic had I not undergone this distinctive trial, or should I say—personality. Figure out what your Heavenly Father wants you to learn. Try to be malleable and humble. Allow something beautiful such as a daisy to grow from the rain cloud of your discouragement. "Sometimes God calms the sea. Sometimes He calms the sailor. And sometimes He makes us swim" (author unknown).

Figure 5–1

When my husband first gave me these flowers (Figure 5–1), the daisies were the same height as the leaves. I placed them in a window with minimal sunlight. In their efforts to bend and stretch toward what light was available, these daisies doubled in height. Often we grow the most in times of trial.

In an article in the June 1989 *Ensign*, President Gordon B. Hinckley stated:

> There are so many out there who need you. It is not enough to work at a word processor forty hours a week and feel that you have done all that you can do. You are needed. There are young people to be taught in the organizations of the Church. Refine your skills. Accept every challenge and assignment. Put time and effort into the preparation of your lessons. Keep your spiritual batteries at full charge and light the lamps of others. It is better to light one candle than to curse the dark.[5]

We can spend countless hours complaining about our lot in life or we can do a lot with our life! President Hinckley also stated in the same address, "You, too, can reach out and give companionship, friendship, love, and nurture to many who are in worse circumstances than your own. Writing of the angel of the slums of Calcutta, George F. Will said: 'Nothing is more beautiful than cheerfulness in an old face. Mother Teresa is proof that a small star's twinkling becomes more noticeable as the night becomes darker' . . . The best medicine for despair is service. The best cure for weariness is the challenge of helping someone who is even more tired."[6]

Happiness can only be experienced if you've also experienced misery. We must take the good with the bad. You will certainly meet opposition in this life, but I encourage you to take President Hinckley's advice to light a candle instead of curse the darkness.

The Lord will not take all discouragement from you. He will, however, ease your burdens so you are able to bear them. Sometimes our prayers must change. Instead of asking Him to take our trials away, we should ask for the strength to withstand them. We should ask, "What do I need to learn from this experience?"

President Harold B. Lee once told an analogy about how burdens can strengthen us.

> One of the mission presidents, with a group of his missionaries back in the Eastern States some years ago, was meeting in a hall with pillars that ran down the center of the hall, and he said to one of the missionaries, "Get up and push that pillar over."
> "Well," said the missionary, "I can't."
> "Why?"
> "Because the weight of that ceiling is all on top of the pillar."

Then the president asked, "Suppose that weight were lifted off. Could you push the pillar over then?"

The missionary replied, "Why, sure, I think I could."

Then the president said, "Now, brethren, you and I are just like one of those pillars. As long as we have a weight of responsibility in this church, all hell can't push us over; but as soon as that weight is lifted off, most of us are easy marks by the powers that drag us down."[7]

Although President Lee was referring to the weight of responsibility in the Church, I feel the same principle can be applied to the trials we face. The very hardships that are so excruciatingly heavy will not crumble us to the ground but rather hold us up against life's storms, *if* we remain faithful and join yoke with the Savior so He can help us through our sufferings.

"Take my yoke upon you, and learn of me; for I am meek and lowly in heart: and *ye shall find rest* unto your souls. For my yoke is easy, and my burden is *light*" (Matthew 11:29–30, emphasis added).

Take Action:

- Remain positive during hardships. Allow yourself to mourn when tragedy strikes. It is normal to grieve after any tragedy; however, positive thinking about the situation can foster an improved mood even amidst intense trials.

- Pray. Pray for strength to rise above your hardship. Pray for peace. Pray to understand what it is you should learn from the experience.

NOTES

1. Spencer W. Kimball, "Friend to Friend: Tragedy or Destiny?," *Friend*, Apr. 1974, 6.

2. Jeffrey R. Holland, "Come Unto Me," *Ensign*, Apr. 1998, 16.

3. Joseph B. Wirthlin, "Come What May, and Love It," *Ensign*, Nov. 2008, 27.

4. Gordon B. Hinckley, "To Single Adults," *Ensign*, June 1989, 72.

5. Ibid.

6. Ibid.

7. Harold B. Lee, "Responsibilities of the Priesthood," *Ensign*, Dec. 1971, 112.

Chapter Six

I KNOW THE SKILLS—NOW WHAT?

I felt on top of the world midway through college when I finally had the skill of positive thinking mastered. My depression seemed to disappear. Or at least it appeared that way for a time. I had learned all of the knowledge that I am sharing with you, and I felt I had put depression behind me forever. Sadness, grief, anxiety, discomfort, and fear are human emotions we cannot escape. So of course, these feeling were bound to come at me again. The first few months after my oldest daughter was born tested my ability to combat depression. The baby blues definitely came, but this time I was ready to handle it. I put the skills into action by changing my *expectations* of perfect parenthood to accepting the fact that I may feel down and disappointed at times. I also accepted that I wouldn't be a perfect mother all of the time. Even though my depression resurfaced for a period of time during my adjustment to parenthood, it was different this time. It was different because I knew it was normal to feel this way, and by changing my "should" statements and my negative thoughts, I was able to stay on top of it. The feelings of sadness come and go now instead of lingering as they once did.

I know of individuals who have learned these skills but claim it didn't cure them. They think this way, I believe, because they expected to never feel despair again. Don't give up when you feel sad yet again. If your cat gets hit by a car—you are going to feel sad! But you won't feel sad forever. Generally, each encounter with routine discouragement gets easier. Each time you are able to push your negative thoughts aside a little quicker. Now when I feel sad I try and just ride through it. I know it will pass, so I use the skills I learned and, most important, I don't panic. I feel sorrow like all humans must, and then I make it through to the other side. I try to eat right, exercise, and fortify daily my testimony with scripture study and prayer. Don't expect feelings of depression to never come. You are on this earth to be tested and tried, not pacified! Be prepared to combat discouragement with mind over matter and the Lord's help.

RECOVERY TIME

Recovering from depression will be different for every person. Negative thinking is wired into your brain, so it will take time to create new pathways. Some people have been negative thinkers their entire life; others have only been for several years. Some only have bouts of depression surrounding serious tragedies or illnesses. Whatever your case may be, recognize that there is no set specifications or time line for eliminating depression completely. You are unique; thus, your particular recovery time will be as well.

Because you may not feel results as fast as you *expect,* you may be tempted to quit trying. (Remember, try to have realistic expectations. Healing takes time.) Although you may feel you aren't progressing at the rate you desire, chances are, your skills are improving more than you realize. I recommend three methods to measure your progress.

- Include the date and time next to each thought you write in your "thought notebook." Do not discard any filled-out pages. Throughout the day as you write down your thoughts, mark down on the same paper, some type of symbol—a smiley face perhaps—when you feel your depression or anxiety subside. You may have several days' worth of sheets before that symbol appears. After several weeks or months go by, you may still be struggling with the same negative thoughts, but you will be able to gauge your progress by the amount of time that lapses between symbols. For example, when you first began changing your thoughts, maybe it took you three days before you felt relief from a particular thought; however, a month later it only took you six hours to recover from that same negative thought.

- Another way to record your progress would be to assign a number to each day on your calendar or day planner. A 10 meaning you struggled very much with depression that day and a 0 meaning your depression was completely gone. Looking back over your calendar, if you see your numbers generally decreasing as the weeks go by, you will know you are making headway. This is a great way to see if certain events trigger your depression, because they will both be written in the same location.

- My third suggestion is to record your symptoms daily in a journal. Write down feelings (example: lonely, empty, hopeless) along with any physical symptoms (example: tired, shortness of breath, headache). Improvement is noticed when there are less symptoms or less intensity of the same symptoms today than there were last month.

If any progress is observed, your efforts are working. With time, you will become quicker and more efficient at ridding negativity from your life until it becomes automatic. If at any time you feel your own efforts are not enough, please consult with a physician or mental health professional.

Take Action:

- Record your progress. Use any of the three methods mentioned above and use it to monitor your success.

Part Two

THE DARK SURRENDERS TO THE DAWN

Chapter Seven

LIGHT VERSUS DARK

"For thou art my lamp, O Lord; and the Lord will lighten my darkness."

—2 Samuel 22:29

Many times I tried to describe with words the sickly feeling of depression. The best word I could ever come up with was "darkness." I used to tell my mom, "It feels like there is a dark cloud following me everywhere I go." I began researching quite heavily about the opposing forces of light and dark, both literally and figuratively, along with their correlation to depression and happiness.

The word *light* is a busy word. *Webster's Dictionary* gives the following definitions for the word *light*: "To make something visible, to reveal or discover, to ignite something, to guide, or to clarify"; synonymous to luminous energy, mental understanding, or a bright source such as a lamp; required for eyes to see; spiritual illumination or enlightenment; comparable to "not dark in color"; light means to cause surroundings to brighten with joy—equivalent to, not heavy, not difficult or burdensome, or free from trouble, sorrow, or worry. Keep in mind the word *light* can be used as a noun, a verb, or an adjective.[1]

The scriptures expound the definition. The Bible Dictionary doesn't give a definition for the solitary word *light*, however; it gives description for the phrase "light of Christ," which is "Enlightenment, knowledge, and an uplifting, ennobling, persevering influence that comes upon mankind because of Jesus Christ."

My uncle Thane Goodrich, PhD, once told me an interesting

definition for the opposing word *dark*: "Philosophically it's interesting to me that darkness is not actually something as much as it is the absence of something—in this case, light. I would make a fortune if I could design a tool that was the opposite of a flashlight. It could be called a "flashdark" and would make things disappear. But it could never exist because dark is not—it's just the lack of light."[2]

As I read the scriptures I replaced the word *dark* with *depression*. When I came across the word *light*, I replaced it with *happiness*. It gave me insight how to cope with my despair. I then began doing this experiment while reading other good books. The following are some examples and analogies I've found.

DARKNESS PARALYZES OUR PROGRESSION

Imagine you are in an unfamiliar room, trying to get from one side to the other. Pretend that the room is pitch black. You might stumble because you cannot see. You might be afraid of stepping on something or running into furniture, so in essence, the darkness slows or stops your progression across the room.

In the book of John, the Apostle writes, "Jesus answered, are there not twelve hours in the day? If any man walk in the day, he stumbleth not, because he seeth the light of this world. But if a man walk in the night, he stumbleth, because there is no light in him" (John 11:9–10). Now think of *depression* and *darkness* meaning the same thing. Depression makes us fearful. If our world is dark it is difficult to make the next step toward our goal. Think about how many times the scriptures and our Church leaders counsel us to press forward. Overcoming discouragement requires increasing our faith. Usually we can't see the next leg of our journey, but putting our faith into action by taking that plunge into the dark will increase our faith. Why? Because we learn from looking back that all things truly are for our good and that everything ends up working out the way it should.

Depression is one of Satan's strategies of halting the work by paralyzing the Saints with darkness and fear. If he can depress you, he can paralyze you, or stop you from excelling and growing in the gospel. He uses the tool of discouragement often because of its lethal and damaging outcome. In his book, *Feeling Good: The New Mood Therapy*, Dr. Burns describes the paralyzing power of depression.

One of the most destructive aspects of depression is the way it paralyzes your willpower. In its mildest form you may simply procrastinate about doing a few odious chores. As your lack of motivation intensifies, virtually any activity appears so difficult that you become overwhelmed by the urge to do nothing. Because you accomplish very little, you feel worse and worse. Not only do you cut yourself off from your normal sources of stimulation and pleasure, but your lack of productivity aggravates your self-hatred, resulting in further isolation and incapacitation.[3]

While Joseph Smith and Oliver Cowdery were translating the golden plates, Oliver allowed his fear to exceed his drive for obedience, and the Lord said, "Behold, it was expedient where you commenced; but you feared, and the time is past, and it is not expedient now" (Doctrine and Covenants 9:11). What opportunities for growth are we passing up because of our fear?

Speaking of his imminent death, Christ said to the people, "Yet a little while is the light with you. Walk while ye have the light, lest darkness come upon you: *for he that walketh in darkness knoweth not whither he goeth.* While ye have light, believe in the light, that ye may be the children of light" (John 12:35–36, emphasis added).

Christ is that light. His gospel helps pull us out of the paralyzing darkness so we can continue forward on our mission. Believe in His light. Believe that His way is the only way to happiness.

Take Action:

- Recognize and overcome your fears. For example, if you are someone who avoids driving because it makes you anxious, get in the car and drive—even if it is only around the block. Start simple.

BE ENLIGHTENED

Light is knowledge. "The glory of God is intelligence, or, in other words, light and truth. Light and truth forsake that evil one" (Doctrine and Covenants 93:36–37). Therefore, it forsakes Satan and his conniving weapon of discouragement. Could this statement be literal? Could intelligence really be equivalent to light? Could it be that our Heavenly Father's countenance shines with more intensity than the noonday sun because he knows *all* things? Could it be that each time we learn something new a little more light is added to our soul? Is this where we got the phrase, "I just had a *light* bulb moment"? I believe this scripture to be true. Whether literally or figuratively, I'm not sure. I do know that if we feed our minds with good wholesome knowledge both temporal and spiritual, that the light in our eyes and the happiness in our lives will increase. In Doctrine and Covenants 6:21 it reads: "Behold, I am Jesus Christ, the Son of God. I am the same that came unto mine own, and mine own received me not. I am the light which shineth in darkness, and the darkness comprehendeth it not."

Sheri Dew, in her book *No Doubt About It*, tells a story of when she was driving home from a basketball game through dense fog. Her friend's son who was riding with them posed a question regarding how the headlights of their car could penetrate through the dark fog. He then answered himself by saying, "Oh, I know. The light is stronger than the dark, isn't it?"[4] It is scientifically proven that light is stronger than darkness. When you step into a dark room and flip the light switch on, the light instantly fills the room and pushes the darkness out. Ironically, as soon as you turn any source of light off, the darkness comes right in. Light has the ability to push darkness away—is stronger than the dark! So if we can continue learning throughout our lives, then the light within us takes up all the space within our souls. The dark will have nowhere to go but out.

Acquired knowledge—both spiritual and temporal—will increase our overall intelligence, but I wish to place emphasis on the necessity for spiritual enlightenment. In my personal scripture study, I recently came across the passage in 1 Nephi where the interpretation of Lehi's dream is given. I pondered on the meaning of the phrase, "The word of God was likened unto an iron rod."

In 1 Nephi 11:25 we read, "And it came to pass that I beheld that the rod of iron, which my father had seen, was the word of God, which led to the fountain of living waters, or to the tree of life; which waters are a representation of the love of God; and I also beheld that the tree of life was a representation of the love of God."

I wondered to myself, *Why iron? Why not a rod of copper or some other durable metal?* I began searching for meanings of the word *iron*. An article in Wikipedia reads, "Iron is the most common element in the whole planet earth, forming much of Earth's outer and inner core, and it is the fourth most common element in the earth's crust."[5] The article later explains that "iron metal has been used since ancient times."[6]

Such an abundant element here on earth surely must have been chosen as the adjective to accompany the symbol representing the "Word of God," because our day is so blessed to have easy access to plentiful scripture. Also, from the beginning of time, God has blessed His children with scripture, showing how both iron, and the "word of God" have been available and used since long ago.

In the April 2010 conference, Elder Christofferson spoke about the profusion of scripture in our day:

> Consider the magnitude of our blessing to have the Holy Bible and some 900 additional pages of scripture, including the Book of Mormon, the Doctrine and Covenants, and the Pearl of Great Price. Then consider that, in addition, the words of prophets spoken as they are moved upon by the Holy Ghost in settings such as this, which the Lord calls scripture (see Doctrine and Covenants 68:2–4), flow to us almost constantly by television, radio, Internet, satellite, CD, DVD, and in print. I suppose that never in history has a people been blessed with such a quantity of holy writ. And not only that, but every man, woman, and child may possess and study his or her own personal copy of these sacred texts, most in his or her own language."[7]

Just as iron provides an analogy of the large amount of scripture available, it can also be likened to the need for iron in our blood. Iron-deficiency anemia is an extremely common blood disorder affecting 30 percent of the world's population.[8] Iron helps make up hemoglobin in the blood. The hemoglobin is responsible for carrying oxygen to the many cells in our bodies.[9] When there is inadequate iron in the diet, hemoglobin production is diminished and the person is left feeling lethargic and weak.[10] In essence, the iron in our blood seems to be somewhat of a life force for us. So it is with the "word of God," It gives us life! It gives us direction and purpose. It is our lifeline to the eternities. When it comes to iron and our diet, we must not forget to daily "feast upon the words of Christ" (2 Nephi 32:3).

Satan, as he always does, leads us in the opposite direction of eternal life. The "rod of iron" leads us to happiness and salvation yet the "yoke of iron" leads us to captivity. In 1 Nephi we read about Satan and his abominable church: "And the angel said unto me: Behold the formation of a church which is most abominable above all other churches, which slayeth the saints of God, yea, and tortureth them and bindeth them down, and yoketh them with a *yoke of iron*, and bringeth them down into captivity (1 Nephi 13:5, emphasis added).

The Book of Mormon gives us knowledge of our enemy so we are able to defend ourselves. By truly searching and feasting on the scriptures, or holding on to this iron rod, we can better take our yoke up with the Savior. For His burden is easy and light; quite the opposite of a heavy "yoke of iron." The Lord says, "Take my yoke upon you, and learn of me; for I am meek and lowly in heart: and ye shall find rest unto your souls. For my yoke *is* easy, and my burden is light" (Matthew 11:29–30). We can only heed His words to "learn of me" by making the iron rod a staple in our spiritual diets.

I know that each day I enlighten my mind with the word of God, I have increased energy and happiness. Scripture study gives me a daily dose of light to fight the darkness. Deeply partaking of the scriptures is as essential to us as the very iron that runs in our blood.

While a solid habit of scripture study is key, there is much temporal knowledge available to bless our lives. My husband's grandmother does crosswords to keep her mind sharp. I like to read nonfiction books that will teach me a new skill or give me new insight into an unknown topic. When I forget to keep learning, I get discouraged, thinking, *All I do is laundry and dishes all day! My brain is probably shriveling right now!* I feel good using my brain and also the new knowledge usually blesses the lives of my family or associates.

Learning blesses our lives when we make it a priority. Our time should be precious to us, and when we put learning over other lazy leisure-time activities, we fulfill the commandment to not be idle. Computer games or online social websites may have their place, but often times our digital era supplies us with excessive time-wasting activities. Spending hours each evening in front of the television will not improve family relationships or much of anything for that matter. Balance is essential in all that we do. Of course there must be time for relaxing, mindless activities, but try to find enjoyment in learning. In time, learning will become a desired free-time activity.

The person who continues to learn throughout their life will find not only amplified happiness, but a keener mind and increased opportunities to be of service. These acts of service will then return you with feelings of self-satisfaction and blessings from Heavenly Father. Darkness will flee when we fill our minds with light, so let us not forget to *enlighten* ourselves always.

Take Action:

- Continue to learn throughout your life. Learning keeps your mind sharp. Pick something you've always wanted to learn and take a class or read a book on it.

EYES—THE WINDOW TO OUR SOUL

There is something magical about gazing into the eyes of a baby. I will never forget those precious moments when recognition finally appeared in my babies' eyes when they saw me. Instead of a blank stare, I actually saw them make the connection that I was their mother. Their eyes seemed to sparkle, and I couldn't help but get a little choked up. What is it about our eyes that seem to glisten when we smile or dim when we are sad or upset? What do they have to do with light and dark? Well, ironically, they are the organ in which we visually see light and dark. Yet they are also the window in which others can see our inner light. Matthew 6:22 states: "The light of the body is the eye: if therefore thine eye be single [to the glory of God], thy whole body shall be full of light." Oh, how I want my whole being to be filled with light as this scripture promises! Yet for this to come true we must have our eye single to that of our Creator's. We might also try to *see* ourselves as our Savior sees us. We should love ourselves as He does.

In Psalms, David, who is sorrowing for his sins, exclaims: "My heart panteth, my strength faileth me: as for the light of mine eyes, it also is gone from me" (Psalm 38:10). Though we are told not to judge, I have noticed that some individuals' eyes seem to divulge their story. They either say, "I am full of light and truth and I am trying to be a good person," or they say, "I am afraid and I don't feel good about myself." Sometimes they say, "I have sinned." Now this isn't always noticeable; however, we know we are to strive to have our Savior's countenance (Alma 5:14, 19). Becoming more like him is the best way I know how to accomplish this, adding light little by little until our souls glow.

CANDLE IN THE TABERNACLE

"For thou wilt light my candle: the Lord my God will enlighten my darkness."

—Psalm 18:28

This tabernacle of clay (our bodies) houses our heavenly spirit. While studying about the ancient tabernacle, revealed in the Old Testament, my testimony was strengthened as I learned of the correlation between that special structure and our earthly bodies. In Exodus we read, "And thou shalt command the children of Israel, that they bring thee pure oil olive beaten for the light, to cause the lamp to burn always" (Exodus 27:20). This menorah of pure olive oil, commanded in the previous scripture to burn always, was the only source of light within the tabernacle. The sacred candle stick was made up of seven branches, seven being the number to represent perfection or wholeness. Other scriptural references teach us that the olive oil in the menorah is symbolism of the Holy Spirit.[11]

The significance of the beaten olive oil is further explained in Donald W. Parry's article in the February 2010 *Ensign* titled, "Christ and Culture in the Old Testament."

> The ancient sacrificial system included several regulations that pertained to beaten olive oil, or "oil made by beating or pounding the olives in a mortar." . . . Beaten oil was also utilized in the temple lamp stand to provide light for those who worked in the temple [Exodus 27:20 as mentioned above]. . . . In the *Book of Mormon*, Abinadi declared, "He is the light and the life of the world; yea, a light that is endless, that can never be darkened (Mosiah 16:9). It is only fitting, then, that the beaten oil be used in lamps to give light in the temple, just as Christ gives light to the entire world. The beaten oil has another connection to Jesus Christ. Beaten oil has been described as "fine and costly" and . . . was prepared through other methods, such as with an olive press. Beaten oil was used because it symbolizes the Savior in two important ways: First, He is the Anointed One, or the one who has been anointed with olive oil. He is called *Christ* and *Messiah*, which means the *anointed one* (with olive oil) in Greek and Hebrew. Second, beaten oil anticipates the experience of Jesus Christ just hours before His death on the cross: He too was beaten. Matthew, Mark, and Luke provide these testimonies: . . . And some began to spit on him, and to cover his face, and to buffet him . . . and the servants did strike him with the palms of their hands.[12]

The symbolism of light continually directs us toward Jesus Christ, our only true source of happiness. Just as the tabernacle had this sacred light burning always, we too must strive to have the light of the Holy Ghost within us at all times. We must endeavor to have the perfect light of Christ fill our earthly bodies. Referring to the ancient tabernacle, the Lord gave the ancient prophets specific instructions on how this light must burn within it. We too have instruction given by way of the gospel to teach us how to keep the light within us alive. The words of our modern-day prophets and the words in the scriptures teach us how to be happy. They turn us toward Christ. They teach us the importance of having a strong testimony burning within us continually.

Take Action:

- Keep your testimony burning strong. If you don't have a testimony, make the effort to gain one. Don't let yourself get into a spiritual slump. Change up your scripture study when it becomes monotonous. Always work on improving your relationship with your Savior and Heavenly Father.

SUNSHINE

"A cloudy day is no match for a sunny disposition."
—William Arthur Ward

In Ecclesiastes it says, "Truly the light is sweet, and a pleasant thing it is for the eyes to behold the sun" (Ecclesiastes 11:7). Although excess sunlight can cause skin cancer and wrinkles, moderate intake of sunshine can help fight the blues.

My husband recalls a time in college when he was a little down. He lacked energy and motivation to even want to go to his classes. His good mother, worried as she was, came down to stay with him for a couple of days. The first thing she did was let some sunshine in by ripping down his dark curtains that covered the entire window. Not only did this brighten his mood, it also made it difficult for him to sleep in and miss class!

Why does sunshine help? First, understand that sunlight and vitamin D go hand in hand. Speaking of sunshine, Carlson wrote, "The sun's action on our body creates vitamin D—the 'sunshine' vitamin. It isn't a true vitamin, however, but a hormone created in the body through a metabolic process involving the intestine, liver, kidneys, and blood, sparked by ultraviolet (UV) light rays on skin cells. . . . One might say that vitamin D from sunlight is the ultimate environmental link connecting us to the cosmos. Without it, we fade and ultimately die."[13]

Furthermore, low levels of vitamin D have been linked to depression.[14] Dr. Stephen S. Ilardi states, "On average, depressed patients have perilously low blood levels of vitamin D. . . . Vitamin D also has a powerful anti-inflammatory effect throughout the body . . . chronic inflammation is a major culprit in depression; it interferes with serotonin function and shuts down activity in key brain regions."[15]

Amid the disorder of depression is a subcategory called Seasonal Affective Disorder (SAD). Dr. Smith and Dr. Elliot explain, "Most scientists believe that the primary cause of SAD is diminished sunlight that accompanies the shorter days in the winter. For many people, reduced light triggers changes that reverberate throughout their bodies and minds, causing their moods to darken."[16]

Now let's talk about melatonin, the hormone known to make you sleepy.[17] Mental Health America states:

> Melatonin, a sleep-related hormone secreted by the pineal gland in the brain, has been linked to SAD. *This hormone, which may cause symptoms of depression, is produced at increased levels in the dark.* Therefore, when the days are shorter and darker the production of this hormone increases. Phototherapy or bright light therapy has been shown to suppress the brain's secretion of melatonin. Although, there have been no research findings to definitely link this therapy with an antidepressant effect, light therapy has been shown to be effective in up to 85 percent of diagnosed cases. Patients remain in light up to ten times the intensity of normal domestic lighting up to four hours a day, but may carry on normal activities such as eating or reading while undergoing treatment. The device most often used today is a bank of white fluorescent lights on a metal reflector and shield with a plastic screen.[18]

It appears to me that sunlight directly impacts our mood through a series of physiological processes. Our modern day is such that we don't need to spend much time outdoors. We have the convenience of electricity and most of our occupations are indoors. Children are inside playing video games more and are outside playing less. I think information regarding vitamin D and sunlight is Heavenly Father's symbolic way of saying, "We need light!"

If you are not already fascinated by the sun, read the following quote regarding its cleansing power. "In the nineteenth century, the invention of the microscope allowed people to view live bacteria. . . . The microscope facilitated viewing of sunlight's physical effect on microorganisms. Direct sunlight inhibited the growth of microorganisms in test tubes, and after several hours of exposure, the bacteria disappeared completely."[19]

The cleansing sun even whitens your clothes when you hang them outside on a line to dry. The sun whitens our clothes, and "The Son" whitens our lives. He helps our scarlet sins to be as white as snow (Isaiah 1:18). Again, to be healthy and happy we need both the *sun* and the *Son*.

"And that which doth not edify is not of God, and is darkness. That which is of God is light; and he that receiveth light, and continueth in God, receiveth more light; and that light groweth brighter and brighter until the perfect day. And again, verily I say unto you, and I say it that you may know the truth, that you may *chase darkness* from among you" (Doctrine and Covenants 50:23–25, emphasis added). If God is light, then the healing power of sunshine most definitely typifies God's healing power.

Professional Insights

The importance of light is illustrated in the circumstances of a young woman I met. Jamie was in her midtwenties and sought counseling because she had come to recognize that something was not right in her life. She described fear and anxiety about facing even the most basic challenges of day to day life. She managed to "show up" to her job but admitted a lack of enthusiasm for work that she had previously enjoyed. Jamie described lacking the desire to go out and socialize with friends, family, or coworkers.

I met with Jamie during the late winter months of February, March, and early April. She was an athlete who trained and competed in long-distance bicycle marathons. Her training included a disciplined routine of biking 10–15 miles every morning. In the early fall of the previous year, Jamie was hit by a car while training. It had taken several weeks of medical care and rehabilitative physical therapy for Jamie to even walk and manage daily tasks. She had made a full recovery, at least physically. She also recognized that she was afraid to return to training out of fear of another accident. In my first meeting with Jamie, she expressed that she sought out counseling to work through the fear and trauma still lingering from the accident. As we continued to explore her situation, other key elements became apparent as well. As Jamie described the symptoms and struggles she had been experiencing for over six months, it was clear that shortly after the accident, depression set in.

Jamie's body had been conditioned to a high level of physical exercise and activity due to her demanding training schedule. Her daily routine, active lifestyle, and diet all supported her athletic pursuits. With her accident had come an abrupt change to the physical realities her body had been accustomed to. Almost instantly Jamie had gone from riding 10–15 miles three or four times each week to no exercise or activity at all. She had been out in the sunlight and fresh air on a regular basis to suddenly being confined indoors and, for a few weeks, in bed. Jamie's accident had happened in the late fall. Coming into the winter months meant shorter days and less sunlight anyway. By the time Jamie healed enough that she could be out, the longer daylight of summer was gone. Something that Jamie had done routinely for several years was to regularly visit an indoor tanning salon during the winter months. Although not natural sunlight, the body's ability to respond to moderate "light therapy" provided by the artificial tanning bed is similar to natural sunlight. My suggestion for her to return to the tanning bed was more for the simulated sunlight it would provide than for the typical cosmetic effects of tanning.

I only met with Jamie for three sessions. Now that she was physically able to return to the training and activity she had formerly been used to, I encouraged her to jump on a stationary bike 2–3 times a week and visit the tanning salon once or twice per month as she had previously done. Jamie started to gradually increase her physical activity. I checked on her about four weeks after our last visit. She had visited the tanning salon and had started gradually returning to her former training schedule. As the symptoms of depression dissipated in her life, she was more effectively able to face the fear and anxiety she felt about the possibility of another accident while training. Resuming the activities that she loved and increasing her sun exposure was just the prescription she needed to overcome the depression in her life.

Take Action:

- Get your daily dose of sunlight. The amount of sunlight exposure is different for every person depending on weight, skin type, and location of residence. Ask your physician how much sunlight is best for you. Open windows or draw back curtains to allow light into your home or work place. Consult with a counselor or physician about your need for possible artificial sunlight during the winter months.

- Exercise. Even a simple walk around the block speeds your body's metabolism and releases natural chemical processes in the brain and nervous system that promote "feeling good."

- Enlist support. Share internal experiences with trustworthy family and friends. Enlist their support and encouragement to help keep you on track with your positive goals.

- Do things you enjoy. Jamie had gotten involved in cycling and competing because it was something she loved to do. Not only had the accident affected her physically, but she had also lost her ability to do something she loved doing. After a few weeks of easing back into her activity, Jamie discovered how much she had missed riding and realized why she started in the first place. Somewhere along the line, you may have dropped hobbies or interests you used to love. Make the time to do something you enjoy.

NOTES

1. *Webster's Unabridged Dictionary: 2nd Edition* (New York, NY: Random House, 1998), 1112.

2. T. Goodrich, personal communication, February 2012.

3. Burns, *Feeling Good*, 81.

4. Sheri L. Dew, *No Doubt About It* (Salt Lake City, UT: Deseret Book, 2001), 15–16.

5. "Iron," *Wikipedia*, the Free Encyclopedia. Wikimedia Foundation, last modified March 18, 2012, http://en.wikipedia.org/wiki/Iron.

6. Ibid.

7. D. Todd Christofferson, "The Blessing of Scripture," *Liahona*, May 2010, 32–35.

8. Lewis, *Medical-Surgical Nursing*, 709.

9. Ibid., 688.

10. Ibid., 709.

11. *Old Testament Student Manuel: Genesis–2 Samuel* (Salt Lake City, Utah: The Church of Jesus Christ of Latter-day Saints, 2003), 149–150.

12. Donald W. Parry, "Christ and Culture In The Old Testament," *Ensign*, Feb. 2010, 55, 56.

13. Laurie W. Carlson, *The Sunlight Solution: Why More Sun Exposure and Vitamin D Are Essential to Your Health* (Amherst, NY: Prometheus Books, 2009), 13.

14. Ibid., 70.

15. Ilardi, *The Depression Cure*, 157.

16. Laura L. Smith, PhD, and Charles H. Elliott, PhD, *Seasonal Affective Disorder for Dummies* (Indianapolis, IN: Wiley Publishing, 2007), 9.

17. Ibid., 38.

18. "Factsheet: Seasonal Affective Disorder (SAD)," Mental Health America, accessed December 7, 2009, http://www.mentalhealthamerica.net/index. cfm?objectid=C7DF957C-1372-4D20-C870C55B099C85EA. Emphasis added.

19. Smith and Elliott, *Seasonal Affective Disorder for Dummies*, 28.

Chapter Eight

EXAMPLES

Is it any wonder, in an increasingly evil world in which we live, that Satan has resorted to such a sneaky and conniving weapon as depression? He realizes perfectly that if you destroy the hope and drive in a person, they might eventually cave. As mentioned before you cannot press forward if you are in the dark. Satan knows this, and he knows he can diminish the growth of God's kingdom and our own progression. He would fill us with darkness to broaden the gap between us and our Heavenly Father, because in God there is no darkness, or sadness (1 John 1:5). Who understands light and dark? There are numerous great examples in the scriptures that we can learn from.

JOB

Wouldn't you say that if anyone had reason to be depressed, it would be the Prophet Job? The guy had it rough! His property and family were destroyed before his eyes. Even his physical body was tormented with boils. It seemed that everything horrible and unimaginable was heaped upon this one man and yet he exclaimed, "Hold your peace, let me alone, that I may speak, and let come on me what will. Wherefore do I take my flesh in my teeth, and put my life in mine hand? Though he slay me, yet will I trust in him: but I will maintain mine own ways before him" (Job 13:13–15). The faith of Job is an amazing motivator to me to trust God always and to bear with dignity whatever comes my way. Job must have felt this darkness but also the light because he spoke often about it.

Job teaches us some important truths. First, he explains how wickedness robs the light from within us. Second, he is another witness that darkness, fear, and depression cause us to lose our purpose. Third, he teaches us that with the Lord's help and with faith in Him, we can endure anything.

Job says, "Yea, the light of the wicked shall be put out, and the spark of his fire shall not shine. The light shall be dark in his tabernacle, and his candle shall be put out with him" (Job 18:5–6). In a later chapter in Job, he explains, "The murderer rising with the light killeth the poor and needy, and in the night is as a thief. The eye also of the adulterer waiteth for the twilight, saying, No eye shall see me: and disguiseth his face. In the dark they dig through houses, which they had marked for themselves in the daytime: *they know not the light*" (Job 24:14–16, emphasis added). The symbolism is double here. Not only is sin often committed in darkness (hidden from the public view), but those who sin do not know the light. This to me says that they know not happiness. They know not the truth. They know not Christ.

In Job 12:25 we read, "They grope in the dark without light, and he maketh them to stagger like a drunken man." Those without the gospel, without knowledge of saving ordinances, stagger with no direction. Those who allow fear and depression to hold them back from becoming, doing, and living, stumble without a course. It is amazing that when you feel the light you can see more clearly where you want to go in life. You have purpose. You have energy.

My favorite scripture in Job is, "Oh that I were as in months past, as in the days when God preserved me; When his candle shined upon my head, and when by his light I walked *through* darkness" (Job 29:2–3, emphasis added). What first appealed to me is that God did not take away his darkness but rather gave him guidance (a candle) to walk through it. This applies to each of us. Often the Lord won't take away our trials or pain; however, through scripture study, prayer, and simple self-talk skills, we will be able to walk through any given trial and reach the other side triumphantly.

There is another treasure of truth in this scripture. Job is speaking of his earlier life when he was prosperous and had his family at his side. He even says, "Oh that I were as in months past," as if to say, the Lord was with me then but not now. At first I asked myself, "Why did the Lord not light his way during these trials—at his darkest time—when all things were taken from him? Why did he feel the Lord's light earlier, but not later—when he seemed to need it most?" At first, it didn't set well with me. Then I remembered the Savior. When on the cross he said, "My God, my God, why hast thou forsaken me?" (Matthew 27:46). Alone, and left to conquer the world by himself, the Savior pleaded. He was alone, but he did not falter. He completed the task he was sent to do. Job must have felt similarly alone and was so utterly discouraged that he couldn't feel the Lord's light. He must have longed for the previous days when he felt the Lord's love and guidance. Because of his faith, Job knew that the Lord's light is never far off. He patiently endured this dark time, knowing the light would eventually come.

I, like many of you fellow sufferers, have been stuck in depression for months sometimes wondering, *Why hast thou forsaken me?* It is at these moments that faith is tested to the max. When you feel alone and your light is out but you press on anyway. When you feel depressed but you get out of bed and take the day on anyway. When you do not give up hope in God even when you feel abandoned, it is then that you pass the test. It is during those times that you must rely on the light you have felt in past months to keep you pressing on. Job passed that test and in the end, his blessings exceeded that of his beginning prosperity (Job 42:12–14). Don't give up. Keep fighting. Don't forsake your faith. Sometimes our Heavenly Father is just standing back, allowing you to do it yourself. He is allowing you to become more like Him as your faith increases and your self-confidence blossoms from the experience.

Take Action:

- Never give up. Press on even when it is difficult. The light will come.

ALMA AND HIS PEOPLE

Mosiah 24 tells the story of Alma and his people who were in bondage to the Lamanites. If you recall, Alma, who was a priest of King Noah, believed Abinadi and broke off from the wicked King Noah. He took his followers and fled. They settled in a place they called Helam. Later they were overtaken by the Lamanites. The Lamanites spared the lives of Alma and his people, but they ruled over them. The king of the Lamanites gave power to Amulon to rule over Alma's people (Mosiah chapters 17, 18, 23). This is where things turn sour. "Amulon began to exercise authority over Alma and his brethren, and began to persecute him, and cause that his children should persecute their children" (Mosiah 24:8). Amulon even threatened to put anyone to death if they were found praying (Mosiah 24:11). Alma's people were keeping the commandments and were favored of the Lord. But even so, he did not take the burden of bondage away. Instead he said, "And I will also ease the burdens which are put upon your shoulders, that even you cannot feel them upon your backs, even while you are in bondage" (Mosiah 24:14). "And now it came to pass that the burdens which were laid upon Alma and his brethren were made *light*; yea, *the Lord did strengthen them* that they could bear up their burdens with ease, and they did submit cheerfully and with patience to all the will of the Lord" (Mosiah 24:15, emphasis added). Job received a similar blessing. His trials were not taken away from him but he was guided through the darkness by the Lord's light (Job 29:2–3).

How are we able to bear the burdens? *Because the Lord strengthens us to bear them*. Like building muscles, the weight you lift is no heavier but your capabilities are increased. "That which we persist in doing becomes easy to do, not that the nature of the thing has changed, but that our power to do it has increased" (Ralph Waldo Emerson).

Take Action:

- Allow the Lord to help carry your burdens.

NEPHI AND LEHI

There is a fabulous story the Book of Mormon about Nephi and Lehi and the miracles that took place while they were imprisoned. First, I'll give a little background information. At this point in the Book of Mormon, the Nephites had become weak because of their pride. Nephi, the son of Helaman, resigned from his place in the judgment seat and basically left to serve a mission with his brother Lehi. These brothers were an unstoppable pair! They had much success converting and baptizing thousands of Lamanites. Obviously upset by this, a Lamanite army took them and threw them into prison (Helaman chapters 4–5). Here is where our story begins.

For several days the two brothers were denied food. When it came time for them to be killed, fire encircled them as a protection. As you can imagine, this event drew a crowd. We are told in the heading of Helaman 5 that a cloud of darkness overshadows three hundred people. Verse 28 says, "And it came to pass that they were overshadowed with a cloud of darkness, and an awful solemn *fear* came upon them" (Helaman 5:28, emphasis added). Verse 29 says that "a voice as if it were above the cloud of darkness," tells them to *repent* . . . they listen. Again in verse 32, the voice returns and tells them to repent . . . they continue listening. The very earth is shaking and the prison walls tremble. Then in verse 33 the voice comes yet a third time . . . and they listen still. All the while the cloud of darkness remain (Helaman 5: 28–33, emphasis added). Verse 34 says, "And it came to pass that the Lamanites *could not flee* because of the cloud of darkness which did overshadow them; yea, and also they were *immovable* because of the *fear* which did come upon them (Helaman 5:34, emphasis added). A man named Aminadab begins to see through the darkness. He beholds Nephi and Lehi, that they are shining, and they are conversing with someone above them (Helaman 5:35–39). Near the end of the chapter, Aminadab advises the people to "cry unto the voice of him who had shaken the earth; yea they did *cry even until the cloud of darkness was dispersed*" (Helaman 5:42, emphasis added).

There are so many wonderful hidden gems in this passage. First, if we want the cloud of darkness to dispel, we must repent. Second, I take courage in knowing that if I wait, and just keeping listening, eventually the darkness will dissipate. The Holy Ghost whispered to these Lamanites three different times, and eventually the darkness cleared. Just keep listening to that "still voice of perfect mildness" which "pierce[s] even to the very soul" (Helaman 5:30).

Verse 34 teaches us again the immobility that comes with darkness or depression. The Lamanites were immovable due to the darkness and their fear which accompanied it.

The ending of this story is magical. Picture being among the multitude covered in this cloud of darkness. You begin pleading—crying out in prayer, expressing your faith and repentant attitude. The darkness dispels and to your amazement, what do you behold? That you and every other person in your company is encircled about by a pillar of fire. It does not harm you. You are filled with joy and the Holy Ghost enters into your heart. Whispers of peace enter your mind. Then angels descend from heaven and minister unto you (Helaman 5:42–48). What a spectacular sight to behold!

Fire first surrounded Nephi and Lehi, and angels administered unto them, but as soon as the darkness was gone, the throng of Lamanites were able to experience this same miracle. Could it be the same with us? Is there a dark cloud fixed around you? Do you feel stuck—immobilized by fear? Perhaps if you could dispel this dark cloud for even a moment, do you think you would see you are not alone? I believe we are always encircled in the light of Christ. I believe the Holy Ghost is always whispering to us—comforting us. I believe that angels minister unto God's children. The darkness fills us with an *untrue* feeling of loneliness, yet we are not alone. Pray, pray, pray even until the cloud of darkness disperses. Turn your minds to heaven . . . and just keep listening.

Take Action:

- Be patient. Be patient with yourself as you learn to overcome depression. Be patient as you wait for blessings or deliverance from particular trials. Give yourself credit. Don't be afraid to recognize even the smallest successes. We are often too eager to dismiss our achievements when compared to lofty expectations we place on ourselves. Don't fall into this trap of self-deception.

THE BROTHER OF JARED

The Brother of Jared happens to be one my favorite prophets of the Book of Mormon. I would love to meet the man that had faith so great that the Lord could not withhold anything from his sight (Ether 12:21). I learned compelling truths about light as I read of the prophet's desire to have light in the barges as they crossed the great waters. To live in darkness seemed unbearable. The Lord agreed yet did not tell him how to get light in the barges. He simply said, "What will ye that I should do that ye may have light in your vessels" (Ether 2:23)? Often the answers to our prayers aren't handed out like candy at a parade. Heavenly Father sometimes wants you to search for your own answers. Also, for most people, the majority of their prayers are answered through the scriptures. For example, three questions were asked of the Lord in Ether chapter two. 1) How should we get light? 2) How will we get air? 3) How will we steer? (Ether 2:19). Two of these questions had never been addressed before in scripture and the answers were freely given. The Lord simply answers those two questions by instructing the Brother of Jared to make a hole at the top and bottom of the vessel that could be opened and closed. He also told him that He would direct the winds so they need not worry about steering. The third question, regarding how there should be light in the vessel, He did not give, rather He questioned the Brother of Jared asking what he would have Him do.

If you recall, there is a similar story in Genesis when Noah built an ark. Perhaps the Lord did not give the Brother of Jared the answer because it was already given in the scriptures. In Genesis it reads, "A window shalt thou make to the ark, and in a cubit shalt thou finish it above; and the door of the ark shalt thou set in the side thereof; with lower, second, and third stories shalt thou make it" (Genesis 6:16). The foot note for "window" in that verse clarifies, "Heb tsohar; some rabbis believed it was a precious stone that shone in the ark" (Genesis 6:16, footnote A). When you are looking for answers to find light in your own life, stop and ponder. Perhaps many of those answers have already been given to you—hard bound in leather, just waiting to be read.

If you compare our bodies to the barges used to cross the great waters, you can see that just as the Jaredites needed light in the barges during their journey, it is important for us to have light within us, or a testimony, through life's journey. The Lord does not wish us to live in darkness.

Dig further into the significance of these sixteen glowing stones spoken of in chapter three. The brother of Jared specifically chose clear, pure rocks for the Lord to touch. It says he "did molten out of a rock sixteen small stones; and they were white and clear, even as transparent glass" (Ether 3:1). Pure glass holds light better than glass with impurities. I assume this is why these transparent rocks were chosen. If our souls are pure and free of imperfection, then we can better hold the light within us as well.

Once inside the barges, the ride to the Americas was not an easy one. Continue the analogy of us being likened unto the barges as you read Ether 6:6–7 which says,

> And it came to pass that they were many times buried in the depths of the sea, because of the mountain waves which broke upon them, and also the great and terrible tempests which were caused by the fierceness of the wind. And it came to pass that when they were

buried in the deep there was no water that could hurt them [Satan could not get them] their vessels being tight like unto a dish, and also they were tight like unto the ark of Noah; therefore when they were encompassed about by many waters they did cry unto the Lord, and he did bring them forth again upon the top of the waters. (Ether 6:6–7, clarification added)

Life's waves will bury us time and time again. But the last sentence of that scripture holds the key, "When they were encompassed about by many waters they did cry unto the Lord, and He did bring them forth again upon the top." As we strive to make our lives "tight like unto a dish," and with the Lord's help, you will always be brought back up to the top. Especially when the waves seem overbearing, I hope you remember the Lord's never-tiring outstretched arms, waiting to pull us up.

Verse ten of the same chapter in Ether says, "And thus they were driven forth; and no monster of the sea could break them, neither whale that could mar them; and they did have *light continually*, whether it was above the water or under the water" (Ether 6:10, emphasis added). This teaches me that I can have access to the Lord's light all the time, especially *during* my trials when I am buried beneath life's waves.

Take Action:

- Search for answers in the scriptures. As you study, have a purpose in mind. Be prayerful about the answers you are looking for. Pray for personal insight and revelation.

JOSEPH SMITH

Joseph Smith, the beloved prophet of this dispensation, made record of a very real acquaintance with darkness. In his own words he says:

After I had retired to the place where I had previously designed to go, having looked around me, and finding myself alone, I kneeled down and began to offer up the desires of my heart to God. I had scarcely done so, when immediately I was seized upon by some power which entirely overcame me, and had such an astonishing influence over me as to bind my tongue so that I could not speak. Thick *darkness* gathered around me, and it seemed to me for a time as if I were doomed to sudden destruction. But, exerting all my powers to call upon God to deliver me out of the power of this enemy which had seized upon me, and at the very moment when I was ready to sink into despair and abandon myself to destruction—not to an imaginary ruin, but to the power of some actual being from the unseen world, who had such marvelous power as I had never before felt in any being—just at this moment of great alarm, I saw a pillar of *light* exactly over my head, above the brightness of the sun, which descended gradually until it fell upon me. It no sooner appeared than I found myself delivered from the enemy which held me bound. When the light rested upon me I saw two Personages, whose brightness and glory defy all description, standing above me in the air. One of them spake unto me, calling me by name and said, pointing to the other—This is My Beloved Son. Hear Him!" (Joseph Smith History 1:15–17, emphasis added).

This was the account given by the prophet of the vision in which he saw God the Father and Jesus Christ. This courageous prayer offered at the young age of fourteen was the beginning of the restored gospel. Of course Satan wanted to stop Joseph Smith. Look at what the prophet accomplished. Look at all of the good that came from his works. What if he had allowed fear to prevent him from continuing? We see that Satan often attacks us with depression when we are at our weakest point, when we are striving to push forward in faith, and when we are about to do something great. Joseph was young and alone, which made him somewhat vulnerable. He was obviously trying to push forward in faith by voicing his prayer, and most clearly, he was about to participate in one of the greatest works the earth has ever seen.

We discover some valuable lessons about darkness from Joseph's experience. First of all, just expect to be bothered by Satan because you are trying to be a good person. Why would Satan bother tempting and harassing those who are already in his grasp? You have made commitments and covenants and are trying your best to "endure to the end." You are doing your best to raise a family and be good employees, citizens, neighbors, or students. In short, you are trying to improve your time while in this life (Alma 34:33), which is a righteous desire, and Satan wants to stop you. So expect him to throw discouragement your direction, but be prepared to fight back.

Another pattern we learn from Joseph Smith is that we should turn to prayer. Yes, his purpose to go into the Sacred Grove was to pray, but I am talking about the prayer that was desperately uttered once the darkness fell upon him. In actuality, there were two prayers offered in the Sacred grove that day. Once Satan's thick mist fell upon him, he exerted all of his power in hopes of God delivering him from the evil presence. Like mentioned before, some of my most fervent prayers were expressed in my saddest hours. We should follow the example of our dear prophet and pray. Pray immediately and automatically when Satan's force turns on us.

You may recall that relief from this dark obscurity did not come to Joseph right as he prayed—it was after. We don't know how long he pled for relief or how long he waited. But we do know that, "At the very moment when he was ready to sink into despair and abandon himself to destruction," or in other words, when it was about as much as he could take, then and only then did the light descend upon him. We will not be delivered instantly out of every hopeless feeling. Peace and comfort will not always immediately come when called upon, but it will come. A loving Father in Heaven will allow us to fester, stir, and grow. We become that much stronger and more confident when we've endured.

Math was always my worst subject. As a young girl, I remember working with my father for long hours in the evening to finish my math homework. I would ask him for help and he would say, "Work it out." This would drive me crazy because he was a genius at math and I knew that he understood exactly how to do it. It would have been so much easier if he would have walked me through each problem step by step. But it turned out that by working, stressing, and figuring out the problem on my own, I remembered it better and I felt more confident in my abilities. He stayed by my side but he did not do the work for me. Just like Joseph, I was not delivered out of my math problems instantly and it only strengthened me as I'm sure his experience strengthened him and prepared him for future trials. The Lord did deliver Joseph as he saw fit. And even though he felt overwhelming despair, it wasn't until the glorious light of God the Father and His Son appeared to him that he was delivered from Satan's grasp. Truly the light is stronger than the dark! It wasn't until the light actually rested upon him that he could then clearly see the two holy personages before him.

THE TRUE SOURCE OF LIGHT—THE LIGHT OF CHRIST

"Then spake Jesus again unto them, saying, I am the light of the world: he that followeth me shall not walk in darkness, but shall have the light of life."

—John 8:12

The heading to section 88 in the *Doctrine and Covenants* says: "All things are controlled and governed by the light of Christ." This heading describes verses 7–13:

> Which truth shineth. This is the light of Christ. As also he is in the sun, and the light of the sun, and the power thereof by which it was made. As also he is in the moon, and is the light of the moon, and the power thereof by which it was made; . . . And the earth also, and the power thereof, even the earth upon which you stand. And the light which shineth, which giveth you light, is through him who enlighteneth your eyes, which is the same light that quickeneth your understandings; *Which light proceedeth forth from the presence of God to fill the immensity of space*—The light which is in all things, which giveth life to all things, which is the law by which all things are governed, even the power of God who sitteth upon his throne, who is in the bosom of eternity, who is in the midst of all things. (Doctrine and Covenants 88:7–13)

Please take a moment to reread this scripture passage and feel the power it holds of our Savior's connection with light. The light proceeds forth *from* Him until it fills the immensity of space! God's love is everywhere. His glory and happiness can reach all. Every creature on this planet is entitled to feel this happiness and peace; this light which radiates toward us. Of course Christ is the perfect example of happiness and light because He is the light!

Consider the following verses. "And it came to pass that the words which came unto Nephi were fulfilled, according as they had been spoken; for behold, at the going down of the sun there was no darkness; and the people began to be astonished because there was no darkness when the night came" (3 Nephi 1:15). Then the contrasting scripture which states, "And it came to pass that it did last for the space of three days that there was no light seen; and there was great mourning and howling and weeping among all the people continually; yea, great were the groanings of the people, because of the darkness and the great destruction which had come upon them" (3 Nephi 8:23). Both passages explain how light was chosen to symbolize the Lord's entrance and exit from this world. What a perfect symbol to use since He *is* the light. Of course the face of the world was covered in thick darkness because His children had just crucified and killed the very source of all light. Not only is He the source but the perfect example of why we all should live in the light.

This entire book could be filled with examples of how Jesus Christ overcame depression and discouragement. He was the only person who was truly alone. He had no Savior to turn to as each of us does. He was born into the world in lonely and humble circumstances. His young life did not consist of social glamour but of mere father-to-son lessons in carpentry. He spent his ministry not in the safe comfort of His personal family, but among the friendless, the poor, and the diseased. His ultimate loneliness pinnacled in Gethsemane and on the cross. And though angels were present for a time, *no one* could deliver Him from the task at hand. Even our perfect brother exclaimed, "Father, if thou be willing, remove this cup from me: nevertheless not my will, but thine, be done" (Luke 22:42). If only we could all approach our tribulations with this sincere devotion to follow the will of God no matter what.

Upon the cross our Savior was utterly alone even without the comfort of His Heavenly Father. He had to feel what all human kind feels when the spirit of God withdraws. Alone. Yes, He was alone. He was depressed. He was dejected. He was disheartened. I'm sure Satan was trying to daunt Him at this hour of possible weakness. But the message we can take from this is that He pressed on anyway—something we can endeavor to do as well.

C.S. Lewis, in his book titled *Mere Christianity*, explicates perfectly the strength our Savior exhibited in never giving in to his discouragement or temptations.

> No man knows how bad he is till he has tried very hard to be good. A silly idea is current that good people do not know what temptation means. This is an obvious lie. Only those who try to resist temptation know how strong it is. After all, you find out the strength of the German army by fighting against it, not by giving in. You find out the strength of a wind by trying to walk against it, not by lying down. A man who gives in to temptation after five minutes simply does not know what it would have been like an hour later. That is why bad people, in one sense, know very little about badness. they have always lived a sheltered life by always giving in. We never find out the strength of the evil impulse inside us until we try to fight it; and Christ, because He was the only man who never yielded to temptation, is also the only man who knows to the full what temptation really means—the only complete realist.[1]

Christ's complete and perfect example of light even lies in his name.

Interestingly, in the English language, Jesus Christ, who is the *Son*, is pronounced the same as the *sun*. These homonyms both radiate light! Elder LeGrand Richards tells us the following, "Not only Abraham was chosen before he was born, but many others of whom we have record. . . . Of all those noble spirits to come upon the earth, the most wonderful, of course, was Christ our Lord, the firstborn, the Son of God. Satan was another and, without going into detail, Satan was a morning star, one of the bright spirits, but because of his own actions he was cast down to the earth and brought with him a third of the host of heaven."[2]

Satan was called *morning star*, and every single day the sun comes up in the east and what does it do? It drives away the morning star out of the sky. Every day! We have a symbolic reminder every single day that our Savior will drive away our foe because His glory is greater. His power is mightier. His love is truer. His light is stronger!

Take Action:

- **Increase your knowledge of the Savior.** Improve your relationship with Him. The more you learn to become like Him, the happier you will be. Strive to develop Christlike attributes. We grow closer to the Savior as we become more like him.

NOTES

1. C.S. Lewis, *Mere Christianity* (New York, NY: HarperCollins Publishers, 1980), 142.

2. LeGrand Richards, "Patriarchal Blessings," *New Era*, Feb. 1977, 4.

Chapter Nine

SCIENCE

Obviously, given my choice of profession, I have a great love for science. I see it as "the subject of the Gods." I imagine eternal classes in heaven where I will learn the exact chemical formula that produces a tree. I think the class will be called, "How to Create a World 101." Science has been known to stray from religion, but I feel they are closely knit and that a study of true laws and principles that govern our universe can solidify our belief in God. I often have discussions with my mother, who is also a nurse, about how we both have felt the spirit touch our hearts while sitting in a biology class learning about the functions of the body or in a chemistry class where we learned how to manipulate matter with heat, catalysts, and the right proportions. Studying subjects such as anatomy and physiology only proved to me that God does exist and that He must have created us. Nothing else has the power to create such a magnificent and complex organism as the human body. And to think—pond scum often gets the credit! The more I learn of His creations and His laws and His world, the more I understand Him. I believe that delving into the intricacies of the science of light only exemplifies the source of all truth and light, our Savior.

FIBER OPTICS

"Behold, my soul delighteth in proving unto my people the truth of the coming of Christ; for, for this end hath the law of Moses been given; and all things which have been given of God from the beginning of the world, unto man, are the typifying of him" (2 Nephi 11:4). If all things typify Christ then light must be included. As I discuss the mechanisms of fiber optics, think of its correlation with the gospel of Jesus Christ.

The Fiber Optic Association describes the physical composition and function of the communication system known as fiber optics. Fiber optics operate by sending signals of light through hair-like fibers of glass or plastic.[1] Three layers make up the basic structure of fiber optics. The core is the very center. This is where the light travels. The cladding surrounds the core. It is the material that keeps the light inside the core and guides it—even through bends. Last, there is the buffer coating, which is the protective outside layer that shields the core from damage or moisture.[2] "The core and cladding are usually made up of ultra-pure glass, although some fibers are all plastic or a glass core and plastic cladding."[3] This allows the light to travel through it. The less impurities glass has, the better light is able to travel through it. (You are beginning to think about the stones and the brother of Jared, aren't you?) Light travels in a straight line but because of the cladding, fiber optics are bendable because the light can just be reflected back toward the center so it continues to travel down the core.

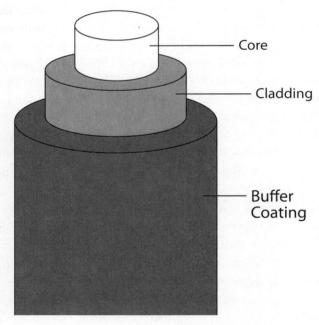

Figure 9–1

Another piece of information to note is that fiber optics are often chosen for long distance communication.[4] Unlike electrical signals in copper wires, light signals from one fiber do not interfere with those of other fibers in the same cable, thus having clearer phone conversations or television reception, or whatever the fiber optic system is being used for.[5]

"There is no such thing as immaterial matter. All spirit is matter, but it is more fine or pure, and can only be discerned by purer eyes; We cannot see it; but when our bodies are purified we shall see that it is all matter" (Doctrine and Covenants 131:7–8). And yet another scripture: "These are they whose *bodies are celestial*, whose glory is that of the sun, even the glory of God, the highest of all, whose glory the sun of the firmament is written of as being typical" (Doctrine and Covenants 76:70, emphasis added). One day, if we rid ourselves of these impurities, our souls may be able to hold the light of a celestial being. We will actually glow based on our righteousness.

How does this relate to fiber optics? Liken the core to our spirits. Although we cannot see them, I suppose our spirits are made up of finer, more translucent material (which can still hold light). The purer our spirits, the more easily light (happiness, truth, and so on) may flow through us. I like to compare the cladding to our hearts. The righteous desires of our hearts reflect the light back into our souls and keeps the light going in the right direction. Also, in my opinion, our heart appears to be a connection between our bodies and our souls just as the cladding connects the core and the buffer coating. Now equate the buffer coating to our physical bodies. It is the outside protective coating that encases our spirits.

Putting it all together, I learn that if I want light to fill my being, I must keep myself pure. All things are matter including our spirits; they are just finer. And if I want to become a celestial being full of happiness and light, I must begin ridding myself of human blemishes.

Another analogy can be made based on the communicable nature of fiber optics. Might the Father also use light as a long distance communication? Maybe just as the individual fibers do not interfere with other fibers in the same cable, perhaps each child's humble prayer does not get mixed in the wash with all His other children. I do not know; I can only speculate. But I'm sure humans have only tapped into the tiniest speck of knowledge when it comes to light and its properties. I already know that the Savior is the source of all light (Doctrine and

Covenants 88:7–13), but someday I want to know all there is to know about light. Someday I hope to know this fascinating mystery of the kingdom.

COLORS

Although science hasn't entirely figured light out, we do know a great deal. Scientists seem to agree that light has properties of both waves and particles.[6] We can only see different colors when light is present. Peter D. Riley in his book titled, *Light and Color*, wrote on this topic. "A ray of light from the sun is made up of seven different colors visible to the naked eye. Together these seven colors are known as a spectrum. It is these colors in light that give color to everything around us."[7] Visible light is only a small portion of light on the electromagnetic spectrum. If we had our heavenly eyes instead of our earthly eyes, might we see more colors?

Black is a color that absorbs all light, whereas white reflects all light. Another quote from Riley explains this: "When sunlight shines on something, some colors are absorbed and some are reflected. The reflected light gives the object its color. A red object absorbs six colors but reflects the red light. A green object absorbs six colors but reflects the green light. A white object reflects all seven colors. *A black object, on the other hand, absorbs all seven colors and so appears black.*"[8]

The basic mechanics of color can be likened to gospel principles. Black objects absorb all light. What absorbs your light? What absorbs your happiness? It may be a silly analogy, but take it for what it's worth. Stay away from black thoughts or things (depressing thoughts, negative people, sin, and so on). Avoid all things that absorb your light. In my life, certain people I have been around do not encourage me to be positive and I am happier when I don't spend much time with them. Pornography, drugs, bad movies and video games, and all other things the prophets have warned us against are black things. They diminish the light you radiate within, thus diminishing your happiness.

Take Action:

- Avoid depression triggers. Learn to recognize what triggers your depression and avoid them if possible or find ways to adjust. For example, if winter triggers your depression, you might begin taking Vitamin D supplements as winter approaches.

OUR EYES

Eyes come in a variety of shapes and colors, adding beauty and uniqueness to every human being. Although small, our eyes provide 80 percent of the information we absorb.[9]

The American Optometric Association gives an explanation about the physical organ of sight. Vision takes place when light rays are reflected off an object and enter the eyes through the cornea. The cornea is transparent and is the outer covering of the eye. The cornea bends to refract the light through the hole of the eye, called the pupil, and through the iris. The iris is a muscle (and is the colored part of the eye) that can get tighter or looser, adjusting the size of the pupil thus allowing more or less light to enter. The light rays then pass through the lens, which also bends and changes shape so it can focus the light onto the retina, which is at the back of the eye. The retina contains millions of little light-sensing nerves called rods and cones. Cones, which are located in the center of the retina, provide a clear and sharp image; they allow us to see color and fine detail. Rods on the other hand, are located on the perimeter of the retina and detect motion, provide peripheral vision and help us see in dim light. The retina then changes the light into an electrical impulse and the optic nerve sends it up to the brain to be processed into an image.[10]

The eyes can only see when light is present. This example of the eye is a parable. During Christ's ministry upon the earth He often taught in parables. Once he was questioned by His disciples as to why he taught in this manner. He replied by saying, "For this people's heart is waxed gross, and their ears are dull of hearing, and their eyes they have closed; lest at any time they should see with their eyes, and hear with their ears, and should understand with their heart, and should be converted, and I should heal them" (Matthew 13:15). Christ was ready to heal them and to give the people further knowledge, but they had in a sense, closed their eyes to Him. They were not teachable because of their pride. What they needed to do was soften their hearts and allow the Holy Spirit to teach them by bringing understanding to Jesus's words.

My uncle Thane explained this same principle with another analogy. "I've often thought the 'new star' of Bethlehem was likely observed and seen by most all people of the world, but few recognized it for what it was—the sign of the birth of Christ. They did not have, 'eyes to see or ears to hear' but nonetheless it was there and they knew it. Seeing things for what and as they really are is sometimes difficult. I suppose depression requires even more effort to push through perceived reality to actual reality."[11]

So just as our eyes require light to see, our minds need "light" to understand. Once light enters into the eye through the cornea, a series of steps takes place before one can see the object. So it is with spiritual understanding. First we must allow the Holy Ghost to enter into our hearts to teach us, then we must have plenty of rods and cones—or receptors—to receive that light. I would wager that the Holy Ghost speaks to us more often than we think, but perhaps the TV is too loud, the radio is on in the car, or we are just too busy to receive his message.

If you liken our hearts to the cornea or to the lens you will see that just as they must bend and change to allow light in, our hearts must be softened and willing to change in order to accept the light of Jesus Christ and the promptings He would have us obtain. The iris in the eye shrinks the pupil in bright light and widens it in dim light. This not only aids in vision but protects delicate light receptors from being damaged by too much light.[12] The way we learn the gospel requires a similar control. We cannot receive all knowledge at once; we must take a day at a time and learn line upon line (2 Nephi 28:30). This method of achieving wisdom by learning "here a little" and "there a little" also protects us as the iris protects the retina. "Unto whom much is given much is required" (Doctrine and Covenants 82:3), so when we learn a truth and then master living it, we are ready to receive more truth. Through this process we are totally prepared to accept responsibility for our newly acquired knowledge. I suppose if we knew *all* things at once then we might be judged more strictly when the final judgment came. It is to our protection and advantage to focus more on living what we already know, then more light and truth will come when we are ready. The function of the iris could also be likened to putting pearls before swine (Matthew 7:6). Gospel truths are precious to us and so we teach them one at a time and only to those who are prepared to ensure that their sacred nature remains undefiled or mocked.

The optic nerve sends impulses to our brain where an image is created. We also know that the Spirit speaks to us both in our heart and our mind (Doctrine and Covenants 8:2). As we change our heart to let the light of Christ in, we will be able to see things, or understand things, that may help us overcome depression. The mechanics of the eye are just another illustration of Jesus Christ's light.

SPEED OF LIGHT

The actual speed of light is approximately 300,000 kilometers per second.[13] To put that in perspective, Wikipedia states, "By every day standards, light travels very rapidly, fast enough to circle the Earth more than 7 times in one second. The speed of light is so great that light can for many practical purposes be regarded as traveling instantaneously."[14] The high-speed power of light is incredible. Wherever light goes it makes darkness disappear immediately. John 1:5 says, "And the light shineth in darkness; and the darkness comprehended it not."

In fighting depression you must not let your light go out because the dark will immediately come in. Remember the light switch example? When you flip the light switch off in a room, darkness takes over. There is no in-between. Elder Hales said it perfectly,

> As children, we learned how to keep darkness away by turning on a light. Sometimes, when our parents went away for the evening, we would turn on every light in the house! We understood the physical law that is also a spiritual law: light and darkness cannot occupy the same space at the same time. Light dispels darkness. When light is present, darkness is vanquished and must depart. More importantly, darkness cannot conquer light unless the light is diminished or departs. When the spiritual light of the Holy Ghost is present, the darkness of Satan departs. Beloved young men and young women of the Church, we are engaged in a battle between the forces of light and darkness. If it were not for the Light of Jesus Christ and His gospel, we would be doomed to the destruction of darkness. But the Savior said, "I am come a light into the world." "He that followeth me shall not walk in darkness, but shall have the light of life."[15]

When you feel signs of depression, quickly correct it with skills you have learned before it escalates. It is easier to add a log to the fire than to restart the fire altogether.

Probably the best example of maintaining your light is the parable of the ten virgins. Five women were prepared and had enough oil in their lamps when the bridegroom came. Five were called foolish because they had none, and they took action too late (Matthew 25:1–13). Although this parable is traditionally likened unto preparing ourselves spiritually for the Second Coming. It also outlines principles to follow when seeking happiness.

When I keep my light burning, one drop of oil at a time and one day at a time, I don't find myself stuck in the lowest hole of depression. If I make little negative thought corrections every day, then I find myself in a state of peace and happiness much of the time. Aside from fighting depression we should be proactive by increasing our light each day. Along with adding oil to your lamp by spiritual obedience, add volume to your light (happiness) by doing little things here and there that you enjoy. One thing that refills my lamp is taking a bubble bath. I also feel recharged by exercising, sewing, or baking. You don't have to be selfish, and you don't have to spend money, but you can take some time for yourself to recharge your spirits. This is a great way to stay on top of the ever-nagging depression. You will have more love and light to offer others if you keep your own lamp full.

Take Action:

- Learn to recognize early signs of depression in yourself. Make necessary corrections to prevent your depression from escalating.

- Do things you enjoy. Reconnect with enjoyable hobbies. Take time for yourself.

DARK ENERGY

A new and mysterious discovery in science is the theory of "dark energy." Only known to scientists for approximately ten years, this energy has only recently been studied in depth.

In her book, *Einstein's Telescope*, Evelyn Gates wrote: "The Universe is expanding ever faster toward an unknown future, powered by something that has been dubbed *dark energy*, whose existence was unexpected and whose presence remains unexplained. Gravity, once thought to be the dominant player on the grand scales of the Universe, is ceding control of the cosmos to this unknown and unseen substance."[16] So the universe is expanding. This doesn't make sense based on gravity alone—which pulls things inwardly toward the sun. This newly discovered dark energy resists gravity.

I am not a cosmologist, but I have learned that there is opposition in all things. Apparently gravity is no exception. Dark energy could be symbolic of Satan's force upon us. Dark energy opposes gravity—something that actually keeps us on the ground. Satan is continually pulling us away from a grounded foundation in Christ. Standing in holy places becomes extremely difficult the more we allow Satan to have hold on us.

In the same book, Gates tells of Albert Einstein's experiments on gravity, some of which reveal some interesting facts on light. As part of his Gedanken experiment using lasers and a box, Einstein found that light responds to gravity just as any other object would.[17] Gates also writes, "Light, which has no mass, is pure energy."[18] Light is not a mass but rather an energy, yet gravity affects it. So it makes sense to me that dark energy, which opposes gravity, is dragging light away from us.

Dark energy is not fully understood, but it does exist. The thought of its existence haunts me, yet I take comfort in knowing that it is not winning in the pull against our light. I can still see the sun shining when I look out my window. The light is stronger than the dark. "The gravitational pull of the Sun's mass is tugging inward on each of the planets in the Solar System, *pulling them in toward the Sun.*"[19] Satan may be using all of his creative tactics on us but we are also being pulled toward the Son of God. All things in this world typify of Him and point us toward Him. The love of God motivates us to return home to Him. We have been blessed with prophets and the restored gospel to pull us toward our Savior.

Avoid whatever your "dark energy" may be as if your planet's stability depended on it! Whether it be pornography, bad music, or negative thoughts. As you hold tight to the iron rod, your gravity will be stable and Satan will have no power to drag the light away from you.

NOTES

1. Jim Hayes, *The FOA Reference Guide to Fiber Optics: A Study Guide to FOA Certification* (Fallbrook, CA: The Fiber Optic Association, 2009), 45.

2. Ibid.

3. Ibid., 46.

4. Ibid., 10, 27.

5. Ibid.

6. Jonathan Orsay, *MCAT Physics,* Seventh Edition (New Jersey: Osote Publishing, 2007), 140.

7. Peter D. Riley, *Light and Color* (Danbury, CT: Franklin Watts, 1999), 18.

8. Ibid., 19, emphasis added.

9. Kent M. Van De Graaff, PhD, "Sensory Organs," in *Human Anatomy, 6th Edition* (New York, NY: The McGraw-Hill Companies, 2002), 499.

10. "How Your Eyes Work," American Optometric Association, 2006–2012, accessed Dec. 8, 2009, http://www.aoa.org/x6024.xml.

11. T. Goodrich, personal communication, February 2012.

12. David Macaulay, *The Way We Work: Getting to Know the Amazing Human Body* (New York, NY: Houghton Mifflin Company, 2008), 175.

13. Peter D. Riley, *Light and Color* (Danbury, Connecticut: Franklin Watts, 1999),6.

14. "The Speed of Light," *Wikipedia*, The Free Encyclopedia. Wikimedia Foundation, accessed August 13, 2009, from http://en.wikipedia.org/wiki/Speed_of_Light.

15. Robert D. Hales, "Out of Darkness into His Marvelous Light," *Liahona*, July 2002, 77.

16. Evelyn Gates, *Einstein's Telescope: The Hunt for Dark Matter and Dark Energy in the Universe* (New York, NY: W. W. Norton & Company, 2009), 4.

17. Ibid., 47.

18. Ibid., 35.

19. Ibid., 93, emphasis added.

Chapter Ten

LET YOUR LIGHT SO SHINE

Our deepest fear is not that we are inadequate. Our deepest fear is that we are powerful beyond measure. It is our light, not our darkness, that most frightens us. We ask ourselves, Who am I to be brilliant, gorgeous, talented, fabulous? Actually, who are you not to be? You are a child of God. Your playing small does not serve the world. There is nothing enlightened about shrinking so that other people won't feel insecure around you. We are all meant to shine, as children do. We were born to make manifest the glory of God that is within us. It's not just in some of us; it's in everyone. And as we let our own light shine, we unconsciously give other people permission to do the same. As we are liberated from our own fear, our presence automatically liberates others.[1]

—Marianne Williamson

Keeping yourself busy by being "anxiously engaged in a good cause," uses up your extra adrenaline—adrenaline left over from all those anxious thoughts. This is best done by serving others, which will make it difficult for you to dwell on your sadness. And whether you actively try to be an example or not, people are watching you. Many people outside the LDS faith observe us as being a "happy people." Maybe this is because we have the truth, and we are a service-oriented people.

You may feel that you don't have enough light yourself, let alone enough light to share with others, but it is in the sharing of your light that more is received. Do His will and glorify God even though you may feel your light is dim and inadequate. His light will shine through you and your example will attract others to this wonderful gospel you possess. It is in the act of doing His will—serving His children—that happiness will come to you. Everyone needs to be needed. If you think, *No one needs me,* you will feel despair. So find someone to need you. Volunteer at a care center, babysit, help a neighbor, call someone who is alone and sad instead of waiting for someone to call you. Then your thoughts will change to, *I just made that person's day.* You will then feel empowered and needed.

Marion D. Hanks, a General Authority in The Church of Jesus Christ of Latter-day Saints once said,

> The Lord said, speaking of His servants, "Their arm shall be my arm" (Doctrine and Covenants 35:14). Have you thought about this? To me this is one of the most sacred and significant and personal commissions I can read about in the holy records or elsewhere. The Lords says this arm of mine is His arm. This mind, this tongue, these hands, these feet, this purse—these are the only tools He has to work with so far as I am concerned . . . So far as you are concerned, your arm, your resources, your intelligence, your tongue, your energy, are the only tools the Lord has to work with.[2]

Knowing God needs you—needs you to do what He cannot do because He is physically not present, should leave you feeling important, wanted, and loved.

President Spencer W. Kimball, a great example of service, also spoke on the matter: "God does notice us, and he watches over us. But it is usually through another person that he meets our needs. Therefore, it is vital that we serve each other."[3]

Depression is bothersome, and most people simply want to rid themselves from it for their own personal freedom. Yet there is another reason we must shake off the chains of darkness that bind us to our own inward thoughts. Depression is such a selfish sickness. It is nearly impossible to help others or even think about anyone else but yourself because you are so concerned with your own pain. We are the Lord's hands. We have too much to do—we don't have time to be depressed! He needs us. He needs our hearts, our minds, and our strength. We can only give him our hands when they are freed from the shackles of depression.

When my oldest child was first born, I found myself fighting the blues on a daily basis. Besides using positive self-talk, I decided to pick someone each day that I could serve. It may have been as simple as calling up an old friend, visiting a widow, or just doing something special for my husband. I began to really enjoy my daily service because it made me forget my own sadness. I began praying to Heavenly Father each morning by saying, *Help me be your hands today.* I prayed that He would help me find people to serve since I had time to give. Every day that I prayed for this, it came to pass. Some days it was just a simple smile to a stranger, yet at the end of the day I could always recall how that prayer was answered. I challenge you to try this. Every morning, pray to be led to someone or a situation where you can help. You will be pleased to find, that day by day, God's mission for you will be unfolded before your eyes.

You are admired by someone. You are needed by someone. Your example to them has made a difference in their life. Even if you don't feel strong yourself, be that good example through Christlike service. Draw others to the glorious light of the gospel of Jesus Christ. As you "let your light so shine" it will never grow dim. As you give what you have to others, you will only gain more yourself. A candle that lights another candle, and another, and another never grows less bright by sharing its flame.

Take Action:

- Increase your service to others. **Your happiness will increase as you bring happiness to those you serve.**

NOTES

1. Marianne Williamson, *A Return to Love: Reflections on the Principles of "A Course in Miracles"* (New York, NY: HarperCollins Publishers, 1992), 165.

2. Marion D. Hanks, *Aaronic Priesthood: Manuel 3.* "Service to Others," (Intellectual Reserve, 1995), 178.

3. Spencer W. Kimball, "The Abundant Life," *Liahona*, June 1979, 3.

Chapter Eleven

SUCCOR ME

Sometimes bad things happen to us because we bring them upon ourselves, sometimes they happen to us as a result of others' actions, and sometimes bad things happen simply because we live in mortality and God chooses not to take trials away in order to test us. By faithfully enduring our trials, we prove to our Heavenly Father that we are worthy of His blessing of eternal life. Doctrine and Covenants 58:2–4 says,

> For verily I say unto you, blessed is he that keepeth my commandments, whether in life or in death; and he that is faithful in tribulation, the reward of the same is greater in the kingdom of heaven. Ye cannot behold with your natural eyes, for the present time, the design of your God concerning those things which shall come hereafter, and the glory which shall follow after much tribulation. For after much tribulation come the blessings. Wherefore the day cometh that ye shall be crowned with much glory; the hour is not yet, but is nigh at hand.

It would be a lie if I said that I welcomed each depressing moment by saying, "Wahoo! Another opportunity for growth, a chance to demonstrate my faith and earn my reward!" I don't say it or even think it. But each trial can be just that, a chance for growth. I feel blessed that I have found ways to overcome my depression but the amazing thing is, even if it were to be my shadow all the days of my life, if I can just endure it, then I can have the greatest blessing ever—eternal life! This is serious motivation to keep fighting.

Most likely you have all had the Sunday School lesson about the string with a knot in the middle. The knot represents this earthly life and the string preceding represents the preexistence, while the string following the knot represents life after death. Although our trials may seem long they truly are short compared to what there is to come. I hope I can have the faith and conviction of Job and other past and present examples who say steadfastly, "No matter what comes, I will not deny the faith." Just as an alcoholic refuses that drink day after day throughout his whole life and comes out in the end victorious, depression must be fought daily if necessary. I don't believe we are judged on the trial we are given but more on how we deal with the trial. Do we curse God and become bitter, or do we endure to the end with faith and diligence? Sometimes I can almost picture God watching us as we meet a trial with a poor attitude. He probably thinks, *Well . . . I'll give her a little more time, let her go to a few more church meetings, and maybe she will handle the next trial more faithfully.* He is always rooting for us, hoping we meet our obstacles with the faith that we say we have.

The thought of enduring this dark road of discouragement may seem bleak and nearly impossible, if not long and lonely; however, we have been taught that we need not travel it alone. Our Savior is walking right beside us every step of the way. He can guide you through anything because He has been through it Himself. He will take your hand and pull you through the hard times. But it is up to each of us to reach up and take His outstretched hand.

Many times the scriptures have brought comfort to me when I needed serious consoling. Two of my favorites are Doctrine and Covenants 121:7–8, which reads, "My son, peace be unto thy soul; thine adversity and thine afflictions shall be but a small moment; And then, if thou endure it well, God shall exalt thee on high; thou shalt triumph over all they foes." The other is Alma 7:12, which says, "And he will take upon him death, that he may loose the bands of death which bind his people; and he will take upon him their infirmities, that his bowels may be filled with mercy, according to the flesh, that he may know according to the flesh how to succor his people according to their infirmities." I do not claim to understand the Atonement fully, but I do know that the Savior voluntarily suffered not only for my sins but for all of my infirmities—including depression. In the flesh He felt what I feel. In fact, He felt worse than I have felt, because he descended below us all (Doctrine and Covenants 122:8).

Elder Jeffrey R. Holland spoke about Christ succoring his people:

Let me quote the marvelous Elder James E. Talmage of the Quorum of the Twelve Apostles on this matter: "Into every adult human life come experiences like unto the battling of the storm-tossed voyagers with contrary winds and threatening sea; ofttimes the night of struggle and danger is far advanced before succor appears; and then, too frequently the saving aid is mistaken for a greater terror. [But,] as came unto [these disciples] in the midst of turbulent waters, so comes to all who toil in faith, the voice of the Deliverer—'It is I; be not afraid;'" (*Jesus the Christ* [1916], 337).

Elder Talmage used the word *succor*. Do you know its meaning? It is used often in the scriptures to describe Christ's care for and attention to us. It means literally "to run to." What a magnificent way to describe the Savior's urgent effort in our behalf! Even as he calls us to come to him and follow him, he is unfailingly running to help us.[1]

Because Christ experienced what we experience, He can succor us perfectly. I remember a couple days after my grandma died, people began bringing meals and things over to the house. One woman, who had recently lost her husband, brought over paper plates, paper cups, and plastic utensils. Usually people brought casseroles or cookies, but this woman remembered the pile of dishes looming in the sink that she just did not have energy to clean during those difficult times after her husband's passing. Because she had experienced a death in the family, she knew first-hand how to help us. She knew that while having food brought over was nice, it was also lovely to have something to eat it on as well.

I also remember a time late in my pregnancy. I was lying there in bed quite miserable with my first sinus infection (and unable to take medication because I was pregnant). I had my head propped up with a fluffy pillow, trying to keep my head from exploding! I thought, "I will never roll my eyes again at a whiney patient who is suffering from a sinus infection." I never knew they could be so miserable until I experienced it myself.

I would be the most amazing nurse in the world if I could experience each of my patient's ailments. I would know exactly how to meet their needs; however, I would not be able to conquer such a challenge before death would defeat me. Only the Infinite One, our Savior, would and could accept this great task (Alma 34:10). He took it upon Himself because He loves us, and He wanted to know exactly how we felt and what we had to go through so that He would know how to comfort us and buoy us up. He could have just suffered for our sins to get the job done, right? But He wanted to experience our experiences. With that said, why is it that He knows better than anyone what we need and yet we forget to call upon His comfort? Our Father in Heaven and His Son know exactly what we need to get through a difficult time. They can comfort us like no one else can. Jesus Christ can bestow tender mercies upon us that are unique to our circumstance. I have had many of these tender mercies, some too precious to share. But time and time again, I pray with gratitude in my heart that the Savior loves me enough to "run to" me.

One day we will all look back on our life and see those trials we were called to face. Like in Isaiah, which reads, "And it shall come to pass in the day that the Lord shall give thee rest from thy sorrow, and from thy fear, and from the hard bondage wherein thou wast made to serve" (Isaiah 14:3). We will eventually be given rest from darkness when the great light of our Savior comes to rule this world with all the peace and joy that eternal life can offer.

NOTES

1. Jeffrey R. Holland, "Come Unto Me," *Ensign*, Apr. 1998, 16.

Chapter Twelve

CHOOSE YOU THIS DAY

The plan of our Heavenly Father was not mistakenly called, "The plan of happiness" (Alma 42:8). If righteous choices are made in each step of the plan from pre-existence, to this earthly life, and then to the life hereafter, we obtain eternal life and eternal happiness. A key principle for this perfect plan to work is agency. We chose to take upon ourselves mortal bodies. We chose to come to this earth to gain experience. Agency is never more necessary than when it comes to happiness.

Remember the scripture in 2 Nephi 2:25 that says, "Adam fell that men may be; and men are, that they *might* have joy"? At the beginning of this book, I posed some questions regarding this passage. I wondered, "Does this scriptures say that men are that they *might* have joy every once in a while?" "Does it mean they *might* experience joy or they *might* not?" I am happy to report that the answer to both of those questions is *no*. The scripture uses the word might because it is up to you. You have agency to be happy or to be miserable. You have the freedom to make your life what you will. You have the power within yourself to make darkness flee and light feel welcome. You have your own will to choose to rise above your trials or to be hardened by them. I hope you choose joy. If you choose to obey God's commandments, to serve others, to control your negative thoughts, and to turn to your Savior, you will then experience true joy that can only be felt when worked for—not given.

The priesthood blessing my father gave me did come true. My

depression did cease. I feel discouraged now and again but I have the power, control, and knowledge within me to make it cease. I am a better stronger person because of this trial and you can be too.

Your attitude will determine if your life's journey will be miserable or joyous. Lehi's family waded through much tribulation in their journey to the promised land. At one point, Laman and Lemuel were complaining about their suffering and lack of material possessions, which they believed contributed to their unhappiness. First Nephi 17:21 states, "Behold, these many years we have suffered in the wilderness, which time we might have enjoyed our possessions and the land of our inheritance; yea, and we *might* have been happy" (emphasis added). All members of the family experienced the same hardships, but those who chose to have a positive attitude, experienced joy because their goal was aimed toward that tree of life, or the love of God, which made them happy (1 Nephi 8:10).

Mormon, a Prophet in the Book of Mormon, teaches us about our final state of happiness based on who we are and what we become in our probationary state. "And then cometh the judgment of the Holy One upon them; and then cometh the time that he that is filthy shall be filthy still; and he that is righteous shall be righteous still; *he that is happy shall be happy still; and he that is unhappy shall be unhappy still*" (Mormon 9:14, emphasis added).

Happiness for some, may be a learned skill. It is one we can make every effort to attain. It is not just the huge events in our life that shape what we become. It is the small choices we make every day that determine our destiny. Every choice made, large or small, will lead you toward happiness or misery. Choose carefully. As you choose, "consider on the blessed and *happy* state of those that keep the commandments of God" (Mosiah 2:41, emphasis added).

Consider the following analogy: The daytime is likened unto the happy times of our lives or just happiness in general. The nighttime is likened unto depression or difficult trying times. God, in His loving wisdom, still provides stars even when it is dark outside. We just need to look for them and keep our chin up so we're able to see them. So it is in our lives—God has not left us starless. There is light everywhere. I pray that you spend your life in constant search of all that is light and good. I hope this book can be, if nothing more, a little star in your dark night to keep you going. I pray you find true happiness as you follow gospel principles and learn self-mastery. I hope you will not give up on yourself when you find you are less than perfect. And most of all, I pray that you will choose happiness in this life and the one to come!

I know with all my heart and soul that Jesus is the Christ! I know deep inside of me that He knows me by name. He knows my favorite color, my favorite food, and that my left foot is a little bigger than the right one. He knows my temptations, my fears, my joys, my weaknesses, and the innermost secrets of my heart. He knows all of us in this very real and intimate way. I know that He died for us and suffered for the sins of all mankind, that if we will but search Him out, He will bring us back home to our Father in Heaven and plead for us in our behalf because He knows just how hard it was to be us. I bear testimony that He knows exactly what we face, for He has faced the same. He truly loves us and chose to save us. He even suffered for those He knew would not accept His precious gift. I will forever be indebted to Him, my elder brother, and my friend—the one who was at my side in the darkest most consuming pits of depression I have ever been in. When I had no one and no answer to ease my pain, He was there. He was—and continues to be—my light.

Appendix A

TAKE ACTION INDEX

Appendix B

WORKSHEETS

1) Write down your symptoms of depression or anxiety.

_____

_____

_____

_____

_____

2) Write down your negative thoughts in the left column. Write down
a positive and true replacement thought next to it in the right column.

Negative Thoughts	Positive Replacement Thoughts

3) Write down your "I should" statements.

I should _____
I should _____
I should _____
I should _____
I should _____
I should _____
I should _____
I should _____
I should _____
I should _____
I should _____
I should _____
I should _____
I should _____
I should _____
I should _____
I should _____
I should _____
I should _____
I should _____
I should _____
I should _____
I should _____
I should _____
I should _____
I should _____
I should _____
I should _____
I should _____
I should _____
I should _____
I should _____
I should _____
I should _____
I should _____

*Cross off unrealistic or unimportant "shoulds"

4) Write down your expectations of other people or events.

_____

_____

_____

_____

_____

_____

_____

_____

_____

_____

_____

_____

_____

_____

_____

_____

_____

_____

_____

_____

_____

_____

_____

_____

_____

*Cross off unrealistic or unimportant expectations

About the Authors

L acey West, a wife, mother, and registered nurse, was born and raised in Delta, Utah. She graduated with honors from Southern Utah University with a bachelor's degree in nursing. Motivated by a desire to conquer her own depression, she spent years researching mental health. She enjoys writing, spending time with family, playing the violin, sewing, photography, creating healthy recipes, and fishing. She resides with her husband and two children in Wichita, Kansas.

G ary Anderson, MS, CMHC, completed his master's degree in psychology through Utah State University and his bachelor's degree at Weber State University in elementary education. Gary has a broad range of professional experience.

He has worked extensively with residential youth treatment programs and with employee assistance programs. He volunteers his clinical services as a member of the State of Utah—Critical Incident Stress Management team providing crisis debriefing to emergency services personnel throughout the state.

Gary is an Eagle Scout and completed a two-year LDS mission. He enjoys camping, gardening, jeep rides, coaching soccer and little league baseball, and spending time with his wife and three children. Gary has worked in the mental health field for over fifteen years and maintains a private mental health practice, Cornerstone Clinical Services, LLC, in Delta, Utah.